In true Barbara M. Britton fashion, this journey around the Sea of Galilee unearths the humanness of the people Jesus interacted with, and even the timeline of events that is easy to skim over.

I loved the insight and Scripture brought out in the devotional. I saw the compassion and love and tenderness of Jesus in an impactful way.

This book brought me to tears as I related with the people who met and served with Jesus.

The true mark of a Biblical Fiction is one that sends me to my Bible—what a perfect way to do that with a built-in devotional!

This crossover fiction + devotion is perfect for visual learners, as the stories come alive on page!

NAOMI CRAIG, BIBLICAL FICTION AUTHOR

Barbara M. Britton's book takes several stories from the Gospels concerning Jesus's travels around the Sea of Galilee. There are multiple fictional vignettes that place characters into the Gospel accounts in order to highlight the interpersonal relations of people that are peripheral to the Gospel narrative. Each story highlights the emotions and impacts of these fictional accounts. As an example, the woman with a chronic medical condition detailed in Mark 5:25-34 is given a name and her character is developed so as to show the likely emotional toll her illness had on her. Most vignettes have a section on the author's application for the story as well as some questions to help the reader understand the meaning of the text.

This book is designed to reach people early in their Christian walk, or those who are beginning to reach out to Jesus. The author's applications sections bring to bear Mrs. Britton's own life experiences and are certainly a highlight for each story in the book.

JAKE JACOBI, MASTER OF THEOLOGY,
REFORMED THEOLOGICAL SEMINARY

You'll be captivated as you journey with Barbara in her recent Bible study, *Across the Lake: Traveling with Jesus Around the Sea of Galilee*. She highlights stories of Jesus's miracles near the *Sea* by making them come to life with authentic, intriguing characters. From casting out demons, healing a woman who suffered for years, to feeding a large crowd, you'll be inspired as it feels like you're really following along with Jesus. Her own reflections about visiting Israel and the study questions make this a complete experience. I highly recommend this unique approach to Bible study—you'll be delighted and encouraged in your faith as you travel with her!

ANN M. COOK, COPY EDITOR FOR JUST BETWEEN US MAGAZINE

Across the Lake: Traveling with Jesus Around the Sea of Galilee brings the Gospels to life with thrilling, immersive narratives that keep you hanging on every sentence. The stories my mom has imagined offer fresh perspectives on Scripture, drawing us deeper into the world of Jesus's ministry with both wonder and faith.

REV. RICHARD BRITTON III, MDIV., PASTOR OF BECKWITH HILLS CHRISTIAN REFORMED CHURCH

Barbara M. Britton, who brought Biblical fiction to life with her Tribes of Israel series, has done it again with her *Across the Lake* Bible study. Here, we follow Jesus as He sails around the Sea of Galilee, performing miracles to reveal His purpose and God's glory. Through the eyes of those Jesus healed, their loved ones, and Simon Peter, we witness the marvelous accounts of Christ's mercy and grace. The book is an emotional read with thought-provoking questions after each vivid event. Biblically accurate, this study can be done with church groups, book clubs, or as your family devotion.

OLIVIA RAE, AWARD-WINNING AUTHOR OF
THE SWORD AND THE CROSS SERIES

ACROSS the LAKE

Traveling with Jesus Around the Sea of Galilee

BARBARA M. BRITTON

scrivinspire

Copyright © 2025 by Barbara M. Britton

Published by ScrivInspire,
an imprint of Scrivenings Press LLC
15 Lucky Lane
Morrilton, Arkansas 72110
https://ScriveningsPress.com

Printed in the United States of America

All rights reserved. No part of this publication may be reproduced, stored in a retrieval system, or transmitted in any form or by any means—for example, electronic, photocopy, and recording— without the prior written permission of the publisher. The only exception is brief quotations in printed reviews.

Paperback ISBN 978-1-64917-557-1

Hardcover ISBN 978-1-64917-563-2

eBook ISBN 978-1-64917-558-8

Editor: Suzie Waltner

Cover design by Linda Fulkerson - www.bookmarketinggraphics.com

Scripture quotations are taken from the NIV Study Bible, Copyright © 1985, 1995, 2002, 2008, 2011, 2020 by Zondervan, Grand Rapids, Michigan 49546, USA www.Zondervan.com "New International Version" and "NIV" are registered trademarks of Biblica, Inc.® Used by permission.

NO AI TRAINING: Without in any way limiting the author's [and publisher's] exclusive rights under copyright, any use of this publication to "train" generative artificial intelligence (AI) technologies to generate text is expressly prohibited. The author reserves all rights to license uses of this work for generative AI training and development of machine learning language models.

This book is dedicated to our family friend, Nancy Beckman, who invited my mom to a Bible study and introduced my whole family to Jesus.

CONTENTS

The Journey — xiii
The disciples as listed in Mark 3:16–19 — xv

PART ONE
GOING TO THE OTHER SIDE

One — 3
Two — 7
Three — 13
Four — 17
Author Reflections — 21
Discussion Questions — 25

PART TWO
HOLDING ON TO A THREAD

One — 31
Two — 35
Three — 39
Four — 45
Author Reflections — 49
Discussion Questions — 53

PART THREE
FASHIONABLY LATE

One — 61
Two — 63
Three — 67
Author Reflections — 71
Discussion Questions — 75

PART FOUR
NOT EVEN A PILLOW?

One — 83
Two — 87
Three — 89
Four — 93

Author Reflections	97
Discussion Questions	101

PART FIVE
FINDING FAST FOOD IN A DESERT

One	107
Two	111
Three	115
Four	117
Five	121
Author Reflections	123
Discussion Questions	127

PART SIX
CASTING FROM AFAR

One	133
Two	135
Three	139
Four	141
Five	143
Author Reflections	147
Discussion Questions	151
Following Jesus	157
Acknowledgments	159
About the Author	161
You May Also Like …	163

When Jesus had again crossed over by boat to the other side of the lake, a large crowd gathered around him while he was by the lake.
Mark 5:21 (NIV)

THE JOURNEY

I have never traveled to a more peaceful place than the region around the Sea of Galilee. Israel was not on my bucket list, so I was surprised, and a little hesitant, when my husband booked a trip to Israel for our thirty-fifth anniversary. I'm sure friends thought I was crazy about being half-hearted regarding the trip. My day job is writing Biblical Fiction about little-known Bible characters. Surely, I could find some stories to write about in Israel.

I set off on a jet with no story ideas in my brain. A few days later, as I lounged in a boat in the middle of the Sea of Galilee, I knew I had to write about this place where Jesus walked, and healed, and battled demons.

Jesus of Nazareth became Jesus of Capernaum. Capernaum is where Jesus lived during his three years of public ministry. The ruins of Peter's house can be found in Capernaum, and Jesus spent a lot of time with Peter, even healing his mother-in-law.

When you live by Lake Michigan, the Sea of Galilee is not that impressive. I equate the sea to one of the larger lakes near my house in Wisconsin. I could stand on the shoreline in Capernaum and see Magdala across the water. Granted, in the days without speed boats or vehicles, it took time to venture from place to place, especially when one walked or rowed a boat. Yet 60 percent of Jesus's miracles occurred in this small region of Israel. For Jesus, this iconic area called Galilee was anything but boring.

I hope you enjoy discovering stories from the Bible that highlight the person of Jesus. A person who was truly God and truly man. Journey with me as I highlight some of His ministry around the Sea of Galilee, a sea that Jesus calls a lake.

THE DISCIPLES AS LISTED IN MARK 3:16-19

- Simon, to whom he gave the name Peter
- James, son of Zebedee, and his brother John
- Andrew
- Philip
- Bartholomew
- Matthew
- Thomas
- James son of Alphaeus
- Thaddaeus
- Simon the Zealot
- Judas Iscariot, who betrayed Him

Part ONE
Going to the Other Side

Scripture Passage:
Mark 4:35-5:20

ONE

They went across the lake to the region of the Gerasenes. When Jesus got out of the boat, a man with an evil spirit came from the tombs to meet him. This man lived in the tombs, and no one could bind him anymore, not even with a chain.
Mark 5:1-3

Felix tucked burlap-wrapped bread under his arm and climbed out the back bedroom window. His mother packed crates in the courtyard of their home for their move from Gerasa. In a few days, his uncle would arrive and escort them to the city of Rome. Felix didn't want to leave his home, but most of all, he didn't want to leave his father. If he could report to his mother that his father was still alive, she might delay their departure. Petitions to the Roman gods, Greek gods, even unnamed gods, had failed to bring his father home from the tombs and free him from the demons.

At twelve years old, Felix failed to earn enough money to support his mother and baby sister. If his father returned home, the life his family had enjoyed in the past would be restored. He yearned to try one last time to make that dream a reality, even though he hadn't seen his father in months.

Dusk descended quickly. A storm on the horizon pushed a gloomy darkness toward the shore. Half a dozen pig farmers accompanied him on the path toward the sea. The men tending to the pigs paid no mind to the changing weather, or a boy hurrying toward the tombs. Their livestock swarmed the wide path, snorting and squealing as if they owned the dirt. Fishermen, soldiers, and merchants hastened homeward, giving a wide berth to the moist snouts and squeals of the herd.

Felix slowed his steps. Was he a fool for going where the dead were buried? The city officials could not bind his father with chains when his rage surfaced. They banished him to the tombs outside of town. Felix had to find his father and convince him to return home. Talking and pleading with a crazy person was his family's only hope. He counted between breaths to calm his clamoring heart.

A curious pig stopped and nuzzled Felix's ankle. The slick tongue nibbling at his flesh sent a shiver across his shoulders. Did the animal smell his bread? He shook his leg to ward off the small beast.

"Don't be afraid, boy." A farmer approached and urged the pig onward with a bushy-ended branch. "There's always a stray or two." The man glanced at Felix's bundle before resuming his trek. A whip and a knife hung from the man's leather belt. He showed no fear passing close to the caves where the demon possessed wasted away.

Don't be afraid. The stranger wouldn't say that if he knew where Felix was going with a loaf of bread smashed to his side. The farmer carried a weapon for protection. Felix cuddled baked grain.

"Gods of the wind and sea," Felix petitioned the advancing clouds, "you're bringing the cover of darkness. Now, bring my father out of the caves and heal his suffering."

The clomp of pig hooves and the shouts of laborers mocked his prayer.

He followed the herd until he veered off the main road. The farmers settled on the hillside for grazing, but he needed to search for his father among stone-carved graves.

Wind blew his thick curls into his face. Rain joined with the wind to sabotage his search. Why did a storm arrive tonight? The day showed no signs of bad weather. He shifted his gaze from the path to the brush. Shadows from swaying cattails and the dip of a terebinth branch had his heart flinching, and his muscles poised for a retreat.

After a short climb, he pressed his back to a tree trunk and scanned the clearing in front of the tombs. Bones of dead people and shards of pottery littered the ground.

Would his father venture out in the rain? Or was he smart enough to stay dry in the caves? Felix's eyes stung, and not from the strain of trying to detect movement in the darkness. Was his mother right? Was life as he knew it finished? Was he an orphan at twelve years of age? Families buried their loved ones and mourned their loss. His family had nothing to bury. He hoped time remained to save his father and prevent a burial. Tonight was his last chance to seek the truth about his father's survival.

Felix shook his head. The tree branches drooped from their battle against the intensifying rain. He pulled the hood of his cloak tight to his face. Curse this storm! Water dripped from his forehead and trickled down his nose. His bread softened into mush beneath his arm. He couldn't stay hunched under a tree all night. He needed to act like the man of the house and locate his father before his mother claimed to be a widow.

Something glimmered in front of the farthest tomb. Links of chain lay near a rolled-away stone. Was it a sign? He stepped from the canopy of branches.

"I'm here, Father." The wind slapped his hood against his face. Could his father even hear his cries? He shouted louder. "It's Felix. Your son. Come out of the cave."

His throat burned as the cool rain moistened his lips. "Come out, Father. I brought you some bread."

The rain answered, intensifying its assault on the packed soil.

"Father, it's Felix." His heartbeat filled his ribcage. "I'm leaving. For good." He held the bundle of bread. Why should he care if the bread became crumbs? No one answered his pleas.

"Goodbye, Father. From me, from mother, from little Delphina." His eyes produced a storm of water all their own.

Someone hovered in the mouth of the far tomb.

"Father?" The name caught in his throat like a stubborn burr. He shivered ten times more than when the pig nuzzled his ankle.

A form stepped into the dim moonlight, tentative, like the skin covering its bones might evaporate in the rain. A shackle clung to a bony wrist. Links of chain hung almost to the ground. The man howled at the storm.

Something surged into Felix's veins, prompting him to flee. But he couldn't leave. This man, possibly his father, had come at his call. Had his father lost the ability to speak and only howled?

Felix answered in kind, howling like a sympathetic beast from the same pack.

The man knelt and gripped something with his hand. Cackling filled the clearing.

Felix backstepped toward the tree trunk. *Thunk.* Something hit the bark and splintered near his head. He jerked and ambled onto the path.

The man lumbered in his direction.

Father or not, Felix threw the bread at the tombs and freed his hands for a fight.

A chorus of shrieks and screams erupted from the man's lips. His eyes glowed like fiery coals, illuminating the night. His expression did not harbor a father's love, but a murderer's hate.

Hope fled from Felix's heart. He sprinted down the slick hillside toward the sea.

Eerie cackling followed after him, growing louder.

Any shred of the man he knew as his father had disappeared.

"Help! Help me." He sought any god that would listen.

TWO

Peter dipped his paddle into the sea and swept air. The angry waves had lifted the fishing boat unusually high only to send it crashing into their watery fury. He gave thanks when he spotted the other boats sailing to Gerasa. His friends had not succumbed to the storm. In all his years as a fisherman, he had never encountered a squall that made him crave land. Why couldn't Jesus have stayed in Capernaum another day? The crowds were plentiful enough for two days' worth of teaching. Evenings were for gutting fish. Not sailing to Roman strongholds.

"Shall we wake him?" Peter's brother Andrew shouted. He sounded as if he waited on shore and wasn't an elbow jab away.

Peter turned his head so Andrew could hear his reply. "Not yet." A spray from the last wave doused Peter's face. He clenched his teeth and blinked moisture from his eyelashes. Tomorrow they would depart in daylight. The crowd would be turned away earlier. Traveling in the dark placed them all in peril.

A gray haze shrouded the shoreline. Were they still on course to Gerasa? He should know, and it bothered him that he didn't. Across the boat, James and John, fellow fishermen, struggled to sit upright against the fury of the storm. Sea water submerged their ankles. One more heavy wave and the boat would sink.

He glanced at their teacher asleep in the stern. Wasn't his cushion soaked? Hadn't the moisture from the rain penetrated Jesus's robe?

A muffled scream from the other side of the boat frayed Peter's threadbare nerves.

Andrew grasped the side. His paddle had vanished.

"Now can we wake him?" Andrew's drenched hair hid his eyes.

The boat pitched sideways. Peter dropped his oar and grabbed for anything sturdy enough to break his fall.

"Teacher," James yelled. "Help us." He clutched his chin as Andrew crawled to aid him.

Andrew cleared the hair from his face and glared in Peter's direction.

"Wake him or I will," Andrew shouted. His ire was but a whisper on the howl of the wind.

Peter stifled a grumble. It was true Jesus lived in his home, but that didn't bestow him the right to order the Teacher around. Though they couldn't all slip to the back of the boat without capsizing the vessel. He crouched and maneuvered to where Jesus slept. Water lapped at his legs as he balanced against the boat's pitch. Not a thread on his garment remained dry.

He knelt in front of Jesus and gently shook his arm. "Teacher, wake up. The men are afraid of drowning." Himself included.

Jesus opened his eyes, but he didn't rise. Was he groggy from a dream?

Peter removed his hand from Jesus's robe. "The storm is swamping the boat."

"Teacher, don't you care if we drown?" someone yelled.

Which disciple had panicked? The howling wind masked the identity of the fearful voice.

Jesus gazed skyward as if noticing the squall for the first time. Rain pelted his face, but no displeasure registered. He rolled into a sitting position and then stood.

Peter grabbed hold of the Teacher's waist to steady him.

Raising his hand toward the unrelenting cascade of water, Jesus scolded the wind. He beheld the waves and said, "Quiet! Be still!"

The Teacher's voice rang in Peter's ear, loud and assured, like when he taught in a synagogue. Jesus's command didn't hold one droplet of concern.

In an instant, wind and water evaporated from the sky. The sea calmed with barely a ripple. Water receded from their boat as if fleeing the Teacher's words.

Peter's legs almost faltered beneath him. He regarded Jesus and then cast a glance toward his friends. Their mouths gaped as they scrambled to behold the berated sea. Were they all in a dream? Not with drenched tunics clinging to their bodies and soaked wood beneath their sandals. What, or who, did the wind and the waves obey? Men, women, and children listened to their Teacher every day on the streets of Galilee, but who banished squalls? The storm fled at the utterance of a few words from Jesus. How was this possible?

Many times, he had heard a man shout for quiet. Some conversations stopped, and some continued on, unaware of the plea. Nothing Peter had witnessed compared to this power. A power over nature where squalls ceased at a man's scold.

He withdrew his steadying arm from Jesus. The brush of woven threads against his hand gave him the assurance he wasn't living in a vision.

Jesus returned to rest on the cushion.

Andrew came alongside Peter. His body shook visibly. "I can see the shores of Gerasa. We weren't knocked off course." He cleared his throat as if more words were trapped inside.

"We won't get there by staring at the land. Grab another paddle and get to work." Peter urged the other men to resume rowing. His bones became light as crushed wheat, but he barked orders and picked up an oar while he began to paddle and ponder.

His brain ached from contemplating Jesus's miracle. He had seen men and women healed from sores and disease. He had seen demons flee from the sick. He had seen those who claimed to be sorcerers humiliated, but he had never seen anyone, not even the Teacher, calm a storm.

Muttering filled the boat. His friends reveled in awe of this moment. They had shared in another miracle of Jesus. But this time, they certainly shared the same question. *Who is this? Even the wind and the waves obey him.*

———

As they reached the shore of Gerasa, Peter hopped out of the boat with James and John, the sons of Zebedee. They secured the vessel. No one, not a single person, spoke of the calming sea. Everyone seemed jittery, as if their minds hovered over the stilled waters. His friends faltered in the simple task of securing a bow.

When all the boats had landed, the men made their way to the path that led to the Gentile city of Gerasa. Why Jesus desired to teach in the Roman stronghold had Peter questioning the fruits of their labor. As if to mock his decision, a herd of pigs covered the hillside. The unclean animals were eaten by those who sneered at the laws of Moses.

His brother bartered a torch from one of the herdsmen. Supplies from the boat remained damp.

Peter trudged behind Jesus and scanned every rock that might offer a warm place to curl into a ball and sleep.

Shouts disturbed the night. Who would be out at this late hour? Word of their travel plans would not have reached this side of the lake. Not with the storm causing chaos.

A young man raced toward Jesus, arms flailing. The boy screamed for help. His high-pitched wail tortured Peter's ears. The young man halted and crouched behind Jesus's robe.

"Save me," the boy pleaded as he wrapped his arms around Jesus's leg.

Jesus did not move. He glanced at the boy and then into the darkness.

A man lumbered toward the shore, howling and twirling something that resembled a whip.

Andrew leaped closer to the Teacher with the torch held high. Flames illuminated the path.

The approaching stranger did not change course, but his pace slowed as he stared at the fire. His intense howling became a simpering whine.

Jesus didn't flinch. He raised his hands as if he was going to bless the man or calm another sea. "Come out of this man, you evil spirit!" The Teacher's voice roared louder than the earlier squall.

Peter shivered and studied James. For a brief second, he wished they were all back in the boat.

THREE

Felix tasted blood as he gripped the man's leg. Men gawked at him as he remained tucked behind the leader in the front of the group. He inched forward, moving as one with the bold stranger. This man did not retreat in a panic toward the sea.

"That's my father." Felix had prayed for help, and suddenly several men appeared from the shore. Would a crowd deter his father? The man the others referred to as a teacher strode to meet his father. Was the man brave, or foolish? Or both? This teacher didn't seem afraid to confront a crazy man full of evil spirits. Many had tried to help his father early on, but no one could cast out the demons. This man spoke as if he could end their possession.

Felix peeked from behind the leader. To his amazement and relief, his father fell on his knees in front of the brave man.

In the torchlight, Felix could see the line of every rib on his father's chest. Dried blood crusted on his father's arms. A sour taste burned in Felix's throat. Had he come too late? He barely recognized this heap of flesh.

"What do you want with me, Jesus, Son of the Most High God?" The words came from his father's lips, but the voice wasn't one Felix recognized. "Swear to God that you won't torture me." Father's body quaked. His bones threatened to break through skin.

How could this Jesus torture his father any worse than the demons inside? Felix came alongside Jesus and stared at his bearded face. He wore a damp cloak and sandals. How could this man be a god?

Jesus stepped forward, close enough that at any moment, Father could lunge and attack. "What is your name?"

Caius. My father's name is Caius. Felix walked with Jesus. If anyone should be assailed this night, it should be him, for he had awakened the demons from the tomb.

"My name is Legion," Father replied in an awful growl.

That isn't true.

"For we are many." His father's frame trembled. A pathetic cry emanated from his mouth. "Don't send us from here. We beg of you." He, no Legion, jerked. "We want to stay. Don't banish us from our home." Contortions marred his face, or the demon's face, or whoever knelt in front of Jesus. Father sobbed like a child.

Tears slipped from Felix's eyes. Was he too far gone? The name of his father hadn't been uttered, only the name of that evil spirit. He stared at Jesus, this godman. "Can you help my father? His name is Caius." Tears dripped down Felix's face. He didn't care if these men thought him weak. His mother and sister needed a provider. He needed a protector, and for Father to return home and make their family whole again.

"We're begging. Don't send us from here." The evil spirits laughed and cried and growled. Father lurched to a stand. "Send us among the pigs." His gnarled hand pointed toward the pigs on the hillside. The small shadows of the livestock made the distant mound of dirt appear alive. "Allow us to go into them."

Jesus rested a hand on Felix's shoulder. His touch was firm yet comforting.

"You have my permission." Jesus spoke in the voice of a Roman centurion who ordered men into battle.

A gust, like the closing of a door, brushed by Felix. The shadows of the lazy pigs half-asleep on the hillside rushed toward the sea. Snorts awakened the night. Farmers shrieked, calling after their livelihood. Splashing echoed farther along the shore. A blanket of white-capped waves aroused the calm sea.

His father collapsed into the dirt.

"Father," he yelled. He ran and scooped his father from the ground, hugging his scarred body close. "I beg of you, Jesus. If you are the Son of the Most High God, then save my father."

The bearded bulk of a man who stood near Jesus walked over, blanket in hand, and knelt. "I believe He already has."

Felix wrapped the blanket around his father's body. As he did so, Father's eyes opened, and his mouth quivered into a smile.

"My son," he whispered. A finger as hardened as granite traced Felix's jawline. "It is you, Felix. It is you." Sobs wracked his shoulders.

Footsteps thundered into the clearing where Jesus and his men had gathered.

"Did you see them?" A pig farmer braced his hands on his knees and breathed heavily. "My herd is gone. Into the sea. What am I going to tell my buyers?"

The outspoken friend of Jesus beheld the others and shrugged. "Tell the buyers something spooked the pigs. That terrible storm gave us a fright too."

FOUR

Peter awoke to a hand shaking his arm. He stretched and rubbed his back where it had sought rest against a boulder. John crouched in front of him. His fellow fisherman embodied refreshment. Scanning the clearing, Peter remembered the demon-possessed man. Caius and his son sat talking with Jesus not far from where they had first met. The disheveled tomb dweller wore a fresh robe, and his hair lay straight against his head. Caius must have bathed while Peter slept.

"We need to go. Crowds are coming." John rose. "Andrew and James have returned with fresh bread and the boats are ready for sailing."

"How long was I out?" Peter pushed against the rock to stand. Dawn's light crept over the horizon to greet him.

"Long enough." John cocked his head in the direction of Jesus. "The owners of the pigs are asking questions. They do not believe this was a normal occurrence."

"They cannot prove we had anything to do with the stampede."

"No, but some men and women came, and they are afraid of Jesus. The antics of Caius were known among the Gerasenes. They seem more afraid of him in his present state than when the demons inhabited his body. An official requested we leave. And he wasn't the only one." John indicated Jesus with his hand. "Shall you get him to the boats or shall I?" His friend was ever the diplomat.

"Since I slept, I will escort him to the shore."

John headed toward the sea.

Peter approached Jesus, who reclined against a log while talking with Caius and his son. "Teacher, we need to leave. The men are ready."

As Jesus got to his feet, Caius dropped to his knees. The man grasped Jesus's foot. "Take me with you, Jesus. You have given me back my life. I will tell everyone I see how you saved me from evil." A floodgate of tears wet Caius's face. "I was dead among the tombs. Now I am alive."

The young boy's shoulders slumped as he listened to his father's words.

Jesus shook his head. "Go home to your family and tell them how much the Lord has done for you, and how He has had mercy on you."

"If you wish me to, I shall." Caius rose and wiped his cheeks. "I will tell everyone who will listen. My boy can be my witness." He ruffled his son's hair. "And to those who won't hear my witness, I will shout it even louder. I may even growl."

Felix's muscles seized, though not from fear of demons nor the fright of never seeing his father again. Jesus was leaving. The man who had saved him from his possessed father, and who had saved his father from the demons, strode toward the sea.

Felix kissed his father's cheek. "I will return." He raced to the shore.

Jesus chatted with some of his friends near their boat. It wasn't too late.

"Jesus!" He scrambled closer and threw his arms around the Teacher's waist. Jesus embraced him as if the squeeze of Felix's arms wasn't an intrusion. "Thank you for healing my father." He let go of the man and stepped back, meeting Jesus's gaze. A gaze that would live in his dreams forever. "I believe it. I believe you are the Son of the Most High God."

Jesus smiled as if Felix was a loyal friend. Not someone he had met hours before, but as if he had known him all of his life.

He would treasure Jesus's broad smile. The smile of the only God who had restored his family and given him a reason to hope.

AUTHOR REFLECTIONS

When I decided to write about my travel around the Sea of Galilee, and the accounts that highlight how amazing Jesus is, I never intended to start with a man who had a legion of demons inside his body. I was familiar with the story of Legion, but I found the story somewhat creepy. This account involves a man living in tombs, indwelled with demons so powerful even chains could not bind him. It wasn't until I dived into the Scripture that I realized parts of the story were missing from many retellings. The missing parts added to the human story, a story to which most of us can relate. I get it. Demons and a stampede of pigs make for a lot of drama, but the simpler side of this story is what touches my heart.

Let's look at the story in Mark 4:35-5:20.

Many Bible readers do not remember that the demon-possessed man hiding in the tombs, a man no one could bind with chains, had a family. We are told about this detail in Mark 5:19 after the man is delivered from his demons.

We see the human impact of this story in the world today. The homeless population is constantly in the news, and so is the epidemic of addiction to dangerous substances. Jesus sees Caius as a human in need of saving, not as a lost cause. When we view this demon-possessed man through the lens of Jesus's love, we see someone who is like us, a sinner who needs a Savior. This sinner had a family impacted by his possession as well. How often do we see people with addictions and afflictions and remember the suffering of their families?

The man also begs to go with Jesus (Mark 5:18). I never realized this detail before. This man, who I named Caius in my short story, wanted to travel with Jesus because he was free of his demons due to a miracle of God. The miracle was not only seen, but felt and realized. This poor man was set free from all the bondage, pain, humiliation, and separation from his family. How many of us, after something fantastic happens in our lives—a happening we attribute to Jesus—beg to give up everything for full-time ministry? Humbly, I say not many.

Jesus denies the man's request to sail with the disciples. Jesus tells him to do something far more important. He sends the man back to his family—to tell and show and shout with joy about the miracle the Son of the Most High God had performed. I'm sure his family was in shock at the transformation. After the shock and surprise, I think there would be an enormous amount of praise and thanksgiving. Wouldn't it have been fun to see a reunion between the man and his family in Scripture?

We see the fear of the townspeople when the man was freed from bondage. They didn't rejoice or organize a party. Check out their hesitation in Mark 5:15. We see the people afraid and pleading for Jesus to leave.

And lastly, when I reflect on these passages, I grab hold of the name of Jesus uttered by a demon. When Jesus encounters Legion, the demon shouts, not whispers, "What do you want with me, Jesus, Son of the Most High God?" The demon nails it. This title for Jesus says everything. Jesus is the Son of the Most High God.

What did the disciples call Jesus in the midst of the squall? When the storm assailed the boat, the disciples called out, "Teacher, don't you care if we drown?"

Which title sounds more like Jesus? The teaching skills of Jesus are renowned, but others have the skill of teaching. There is only one Son of the Most High God.

In this world, there are many cults that take away the Sonship of Jesus. These false religions break up the Trinity of the One True God (Father-Son-Holy Spirit) and make Jesus something lower in status, like a created being, an angel, or just another god among many. My heart aches for those who miss the Son, Jesus.

The next time you hear the story of the calming of the Sea of Galilee, or you listen to someone talk about a man possessed whose demons flee into a herd of pigs, think about the human side of this account. Remember that a man who fell into possession and lived like an animal among the dead didn't remain in bondage. Jesus, not just a teacher but the Son of the Most High God, set him free and sent him home to his family.

The freed man was so thankful for his healing, he was willing to give up everything to follow Jesus.

"Tell them how much the Lord has done for you, and how he has had mercy on you." This is all Jesus asked of him.

The man was a faithful witness to Jesus's miracle. The ending of this account states, "All the people were amazed."

I hope you are amazed by Jesus, the Son of the Most High God.

DISCUSSION QUESTIONS

DISCUSSION ONE

The region of the Gerasenes where the demon-possessed man lived would have been a cosmopolitan city of Gentiles under Roman control. Archaeologists knew which unearthed cities were Jewish or Gentile due to the lack of pig bones in the excavations. The Jewish people did not eat pigs. The pig was an unclean animal. You can find the Jewish food laws relating to pigs in Leviticus 11:1-8.

We know archaeologists would have found pig bones in the region of the Gerasenes due to the account in Mark 5. Herds of pigs were scattered on the hillsides when Jesus and the disciples arrived.

How many people today are like Felix, reaching out to gods that don't exist? False gods cannot help you in times of trouble. Felix discovers the false gods worshiped in Gerasa were useless in his time of need. How can you share the message of Jesus, the Son of the Most High God, with people you meet?

_____
_____
_____
_____

DISCUSSION QUESTIONS

If you want to know the good news of the Gospel, you can find out what God has done for you with these verses, fondly called the Romans Road.

Romans 3:23, 6:23, 5:8, 10:9-10.

DISCUSSION TWO

When I toured the Sea of Galilee, I saw "The Jesus Boat." This boat was unearthed in 1986, but it was from the first century AD. The disciples probably rode in a similar boat to cross the Sea of Galilee. I can see why the disciples would be afraid to be caught in a storm with a wooden boat from Galilee of old. The sides weren't particularly high, and the boat was a humble size. The structure didn't appear large enough to hold six good-sized men. Perhaps that is why more than one boat is mentioned in the text. I could sympathize with the fear of the disciples as I would be calling for Jesus to wake up too.

Review the story and Scripture. How many actions did Jesus take to banish the storm? Do you see more than one?

Have you ever been in a perilous situation? How did you react to the trauma? Did this story give you comfort? Why or why not?

_____
_____
_____
_____

DISCUSSION THREE

In the other accounts of Jesus calming the storm in Matthew 8:23-27 and Luke 8:22-25, Jesus is called Lord and Master. Those aren't bad names, but they don't compare to the name shouted by a demon. Can you think of other names given to Jesus in the Bible? What are some of your favorites?

_____
_____

DISCUSSION QUESTIONS

DISCUSSION FOUR

While I was on the Sea of Galilee, softly rocking in a large boat, I wrote these words:

No matter where you are in your life,
No matter how small a place that you come from,
Or how small a reach you think you have,
God can use you.
No matter what you've been through,
Or where you have been,
God can use you to shine a light for Him.

During this week, remember a rocking boat and a man who lived among the rocks. Praise God for the miracles and ministry of Jesus as he traveled across the lake.

Where do you see God working in your life? If you are unsure, ask a close friend or family member if they have seen changes in your life because of your faith in Jesus.

If you are searching for the One True God, what is keeping you from reaching out to Him?

DISCUSSION QUESTIONS

Make notes for yourself or share with a group where you saw God working in your life this week. It may not be as dramatic as a storm ceasing or demons fleeing, but God is with those who trust in Jesus, and there is a world in need of His love.

Part TWO
Holding on to a Thread

Scripture Passage:
Mark 5:21-34

ONE

When she heard about Jesus, she came up behind him in the crowd and touched his cloak, because she thought, "If I just touch his clothes, I will be healed."
Mark 5:27-28

Lydia heard the buzzing before she opened her eyes. How long had she been asleep? She swatted the fly away from her face and rolled onto her side. A hint of light filtered into her tent. Early morning light. The evening storm had passed.

She pushed herself into a sitting position and almost collapsed onto the woven mat beneath her. When had she last eaten? Her mind filled with nothing. No time, no remembrance of talk, nor lingering taste.

More flies buzzed near her feet. Not again. She had flooded her rag. Where was Phoebe? Her servant girl should have woken her and brought a basin of water. Ah, yes. Phoebe had left for the women's tent a few days ago. A tent her servant could leave after her bleeding stopped. A tent filled with people who didn't fear being near her.

Lydia tried to stand, but the ground rolled like waves from the sea. She crumpled to her bed.

She raised a fist toward the top of the small tent. "Why do You punish me year after year? Take my breath and end this suffering."

Twelve years was too long to live and watch life mock her. "I've done what the leaders say, and I still bleed. Instead of getting better, I grow weaker with each passing year. Is this a game to You? I'm finished with it." A piece of her heart silenced her plea. She couldn't be done with this world. As long as she was alive, she could protect Phoebe. Upon her death, her brother would descend and either sell the girl or make her live a sullied life. She shivered and patted the few coins remaining in her pocket. What would she do when they were gone?

"God, you may turn Your face from me but provide for my Phoebe."

The girl, from seven years of age, had seen to Lydia's care when constant bleeding had made Lydia an outcast. An unclean outcast living in a tent apart from her family, and from … him.

Her father had bestowed some of the money he received for a bride price. A price she had not been able to honor due to her curse of bleeding. At twenty-four, she observed life from a distance, watching what could have been wither away. She didn't ponder what was lost anymore. Imagining hours spent with a husband and children caused her heart to decay.

Sapped of strength, she lay flat on her back, staring at the same scenery. She had memorized every stitch and stain on the ram skin tent. The need to gather water from the jars outside required her to get up and move.

"Lord, keep me upright in this heat. You at least owe me that request."

She forced her body to sit while she cleaned herself and secured a head covering. Grasping a nearby walking stick, she rose and willed the earth to steady itself. One step. Then, another. Then, a shuffle.

As she opened the tent flap, the sunrise blinded her. No trees shaded her dwelling in this remote field. Oh, if she could only relish the warmth of the sun without losing strength. Gone were the days of racing in the hills above Capernaum and jumping into the sea. She laughed at the folly from long ago.

"Lydia."

She turned toward the low rumble of her name. There stood Elon. His hair was not as curly as it had been twelve years prior. The sun had stolen some of its rich color. But thankfully, her illness had not stolen him. His family thought he was a fool to wait for her, to honor the betrothal from their childhood, but wait, and linger, he did. For a woman who, at twenty-four years of age, was considered scorned by God.

Her chest tightened. She was struck dumb by his presence. He regularly left her food, but his gifts appeared in secret, left under the cover of darkness.

"I brought you some food the night before last. Before the storm." He indicated a basket tucked under the tent flap. "When it was here this day, I thought …"

My death had finally come.

She struggled to find her voice. "Phoebe is gone. No one is here to take care of me." *But you.* Tears blurred her vision, but they could never diminish the beauty of Elon. "*Toda raba.*" She longed to say more, to give more, other than a common thank you. She longed to say she would be healed soon, and they could finally be together. Those days had come and gone, and gone again, until her words were a comforting lie. Repeating the falsehood that she would be physically restored hurt too much. "You are very generous. As always."

She slumped against her walking stick, the emerging heat draining her strength.

Elon flinched. He could not offer her assistance without becoming unclean. As if sensing why she traveled from her tent, he sprinted to a water jar and set it by her ram skin prison.

A tear slipped from her eye and graced her cheek. "You are too good to me, Elon." *And good for her. You should have abandoned me years ago.*

Before she collapsed and embarrassed herself, and him, she grasped his basket and turned toward her tent. The rain had dampened the woven reeds, so the handle fit securely in her palm. If only her future were as secure.

"There is a man." Elon's words chased after her. "He lives with a fisherman. Near the lake."

There was always a man who claimed he could help her. For a fee. The slashes and burns and bindings of the physicians had never healed her. Her health worsened. The horrors of what they had made her drink sickened her stomach. She had only received disappointment and pain.

She pivoted with the aid of her stick. How could he not understand her curse would never end? Year after year, the bleeding remained, deepened, and mocked her, despite her prayers and his offerings.

"I will take you to him." Elon's gaze held an intensity buried for several years.

"What is his trade?" Crazed sorcerer? Screaming healer? Wealthy butcher?

Elon beheld her with an unassuming earnestness. "His father is a carpenter. I believe he is one as well."

She almost laughed. Such a rare occurrence. Though she would not insult her beloved.

"He has cured people of leprosy and fevers." Elon clasped his hands. "Those healed are not known to be liars."

"I will think on it." She tore her gaze from his handsomeness. "For you, Elon." *Only because of you.*

TWO

Lydia lounged on her mat and nibbled a piece of Elon's bread. The dear man had postponed her starvation a few more days. With so few coins left in her pocket, soon she would be too weak to live even with his generosity.

She plucked a grape from a cluster nestled in her gift. The sweet juice enlivened her senses. Alive. She teetered between life and death. Her jaw tightened with a joyous ache. Tasting another piece of fruit, she closed her eyes and savored the goodness.

"Lord." The address to her God came forth with a rasp. "I begged You for forgiveness. From what sin, I do not know. I have sought healing from the teachers and offered the sacrifices You require. What is left for me to do? I have nothing save my last coins. If I am to die, take me swiftly. If I am to live, make me whole once more like when I was a young girl. Be swift, O' Lord. Not for me alone, but for Phoebe and Your faithful servant Elon." Her throat constricted at the mention of her weary betrothed.

The tent flap whipped open.

Lydia jumped as Phoebe raced inside.

"He is coming. Today." Flushed with color, Phoebe grasped Lydia's hand.

"Dear girl, you are unclean too soon."

"We must go to town before He leaves again."

Lydia shook her head. The girl was not listening to reason. "What are you talking about? You bound into my tent without a greeting and grab me like a thief."

"The healer will be here soon. I heard a messenger." Phoebe's chest heaved. "He was shouting about it on my way to your tent. The rabbi will arrive from across the lake." Phoebe blew out a long breath. "Over the past days, women have told me of His miracles. Some say He has cured leprosy and cast out demons."

Lydia's belly spasmed. "I am not demon possessed."

Phoebe let go of Lydia's hand. "Look at me. People are saying He might be the Messiah. God in the flesh. If this is true, He could heal you."

Was this the same man Elon had spoken of? For twelve years she had been shunned. Forgotten. With each treatment her hopes had been raised, only to plunge into despair when blood continued to flow. Was she to believe her time for healing had come?

"Isn't it worth a trip to town?" Phoebe plopped down next to the mat and plucked a grape. Her eyes widened as if waiting for an answer, but that stare held a challenge to heed her message.

Could Lydia hope one last time? Really hope. This day didn't seem any different than the last one. Her cracked fingernail traced the weave of Elon's basket. The thought of being discovered and beaten with sticks made her temples ache. But if everything the women had said was true, this man may be able to cure her bleeding and make her ceremonially clean. Year after year she had yearned to be whole, and accepted, yet she still bled.

"What if I touch someone's cloak? They will be unclean. And I can hardly walk out of the tent, let alone to town." Didn't Phoebe see this was a fool's errand? Done in daylight no less. "My body is too weak and—"

"We will cover your face with a veil." Phoebe leaned closer. "I will help you walk. I even know where we can get a cart. Promise me that you will see this man."

Lydia's mind whirled with scenarios. Some were pleasant. Most of the images relayed chaos and condemnation if she were discovered.

ACROSS THE LAKE

"What if the crowd picks up stones?" In her condition a beating would bring death. If this man were truly the Messiah, could He give her life?

Phoebe patted the mat. "The crowd will be focused on Jesus. Besides, no one has seen you of late. You do not resemble …" Her expression sobered. "I'll make sure my face is covered as well."

The truth in Phoebe's statement impaled Lydia's heart. No one in her family had come to call in over a year. Only Phoebe and Elon had looked upon her frailness. Dare she admit God had looked upon her struggles each and every day? For some reason, He had kept her alive. Would He consider her bold appeal once more and have pity on her? *Oh, God, is this urging from Elon and Phoebe of Your doing?*

Did she possess the strength to believe in a miracle one more time?

Taking Phoebe's hand, she clutched it with a fervor long buried. "I have nothing left to offer God but my faith. If this man is the Messiah, and the stories of His healings are true, I believe He will have the power to heal me." She grinned as a sliver of hope grew in her heart. "I will go with you, Phoebe. What is a little blood to a man who has healed a leper's weeping skin?"

The girl nearly flattened her body with a lively embrace.

"Hurry. We must go." Phoebe jumped to her feet and held out her hand.

Another latent laugh threatened to bark from Lydia's lips. "When have I last hurried?"

With his oar, Peter swept the lake one last time. He dug deep, sending their boat sailing toward the shores of Capernaum. The lazy ripples upon the sea reminded him of Jesus calming the storm the previous night. Had it really been less than a day since Jesus rebuked the waves?

He glanced at Jesus, who conversed with John. How many talks had their small group had with the Son of God? The lips of the Gerasene proclaimed Jesus was the Son of the Most High God. Yet Jesus sat with sweat stains on his tunic and calloused feet from walking around Galilee.

Andrew came alongside him and elbowed Peter's side. "Word travels fast these days." He indicated the shore where a boy raced along the sea. A few people gathered where the fishing boats docked. "It's like someone is going ahead of us to rile the people."

Peter studied the shoreline. "They cannot know about the pigs and the demons. Not so soon."

"Several towns could have been alerted. You slept a while." Andrew flashed an irritating smile. "We cannot hide when Jesus is in our boat."

His brother spoke a frightening truth. Wherever Jesus traveled, crowds appeared, and they grew larger with each healing or proclamation. As long as the people stayed peaceful, there would be no need to worry. If he and Andrew prevented a riot and acted respectfully toward the synagogue ruler, trouble would be averted, and their family would remain safe.

"Get ready to hop out of the boat and secure it on shore." Peter set down his oar and cast a glance at the gathering crowd. "Perhaps when the townspeople see us, they will believe we have been out fishing."

"I doubt it." Andrew indicated Jesus with a tilt of his head. "We're carrying one big fish."

THREE

Couldn't they travel more than a few yards on shore without assembling a crowd?

Peter joined Jesus as Andrew secured the boats. John strolled on the other side of Jesus. John's chin lifted as he scanned the mass of people streaming from the center marketplace. Capernaum was once a sleepy fishing village with the occasional millstone merchant arguing over a price. Now the main thoroughfare overflowed with strangers. Some used crutches to walk and others wore dirty bandages. How far had the sick journeyed in search of Jesus?

Authoritative shouts caused the people to part and form a path in front of Jesus. The synagogue ruler rushed forward. A few of the synagogue's hired caretakers followed in the ruler's wake. The ruler, Jairus, allowed Jesus to speak to the faithful worshipers in Capernaum. Had someone complained to him about Jesus's teaching? Jesus taught truth for all to hear and understand.

Peter stiffened. Perhaps the wealthy opposed the crowds outside of the synagogue. The sandals of the seekers may have trampled bushes or overtaken courtyards. At least he prayed that was the trouble and not a charge of heresy.

Jesus halted and opened his arms as if receiving an old friend.

Jairus stumbled and fell at Jesus's feet. The ruler's cloak slid from his shoulder.

"My little daughter is dying." Jairus clasped his hands. His features did not hold the assurance of a wealthy and respected man, but of a father ripe with fear. "Please come and put your hands on her so that she will be healed and live." His gaze beseeched Jesus to honor his request.

People crowded closer to gawk at the distressed synagogue ruler. Their voices murmured sympathy and support.

Jesus nodded and indicated for Jairus to lead the way through town.

Peter glanced at John. His fellow disciple raised an eyebrow of concern. Was this a true illness or a trap? Some of those in authority were skeptical of Jesus and the healings attributed to Him.

John pushed Peter down the main road from the lake. "I will follow you. Your brawn cuts a wider path, and your furrowed expression will keep the people away."

If only that were true. The more word traveled about Jesus and His miracles, the more people sought Him. Desperate people did not listen to reason or wait patiently to be healed. Even if a distraught religious ruler stood near Jesus's side.

"Keep up then," Peter called above the mutterings of the crowd. "For it seems our boat was a shofar blast calling all in Capernaum to assemble."

With every jolt and rumble of the cart bed, Lydia prayed no stain marred her garment and gave her away as unclean. She gripped her head covering tight, peering through the tassels that hid her eyes and cheeks. Phoebe stayed covered as well, leading the donkey toward the main road through town. If Elon had followed them, she had not made out his form, but then people amassed in droves as they neared the center of Capernaum. Phoebe was not the only one who had heard of the rabbi's miracles.

Lydia shivered as she surveyed the crowds. Most were able-bodied.

They could chase Jesus through the streets. What if the Messiah came close to her but passed her by? What if she was driven from His presence because of her bleeding? Or worse. What if she was knocked down only inches from all hope?

"God of Abraham, Isaac, and Jacob, number my steps and fill me with the strength that I need to seek You." A tear slipped from her eyelash and tickled the side of her nose. "I have waited so long."

"There He is." Phoebe urged the donkey into a trot.

Lydia jerked backward. She grabbed hold of the cart. The wooden side was as warm as the cloth covering her head. The sun had become her enemy.

Men, women, and children emerged from side roads to the north and east. They hurried toward the main route to the sea.

"Someone is with Him." Phoebe's voice burst forth. "It is Jairus. The Messiah may be going to teach in the synagogue."

Lydia covered her mouth to stifle a wail. She could not go into the synagogue. Not in her soiled, unclean state. Would Jairus recognize her after all these years? She prayed his mind was scattered with the commotion at his footsteps.

Her heart sank even further into despair. With so many people, the cart would not be able to cut a path to Jesus. Had Phoebe's urging been for naught?

No. Her time was now. Weak or ill or stifled, she had to reach the Savior. She didn't have the strength to live for one more Sabbath.

God of Abraham, Isaac, and Jacob, hear my prayer. I believe You can heal me. I believe You are here, striding through Capernaum. Somehow, some way, hear my plea. Grant me strength, Lord. I'm coming. I'm coming to You. Her countenance soared with every syllable of her prayer.

She scurried out of the cart and grabbed Phoebe's hand. "We must go."

Phoebe's eyes widened under the wrap of her veil. "I have not seen you like this in years. It is good to hear an eagerness in your words again. Take hold of my arm, and we will make our way to the Messiah."

"I will secure the donkey." *Elon.* He had been following them all this time.

She did not glance in his direction. She could not, for if she saw the hope in his eyes and crushed his dreams once more, her spirit would fade away.

Overflow my cup with belief, Lord.

Phoebe handed Elon the reins and wrapped her arm around Lydia's waist. "Slap one sandal in front of the other and follow my path." Phoebe's head rested briefly against Lydia's shoulder.

The firm ground beneath Lydia's leather sandals spurred her onward, but the motion of the crowd and the heat from their bodies caused her vision to dance with tiny lights. She concentrated on the support of Phoebe and the solid dirt below her feet. One step. Another. One more.

"Out of our way," Phoebe shouted. "My mother has need of the rabbi."

I only have five years on you.

She would not correct her pillar, for Phoebe's words brought a slight parting in the crowd.

Lydia glimpsed Jesus ahead. He traveled toward the synagogue with Jairus. A swarm of people descended on Jesus with outstretched arms, their voices beckoning Him to stop His progress. The men at Jesus's sides kept the crowd from crushing the healer.

Phoebe sprinted forward, tugging Lydia closer. Closer to Jesus. So close. The rabbi's profile relaxed as He nodded at those around Him. No frustration or disgust showed on His face, unlike the men trying to control the multitudes.

Shouts and summons of the desperate townspeople filled Lydia's ears. A woman jostled her, elbowing her in the side. *If she only knew.*

"Out of my way," the woman shrieked.

Phoebe held her ground and kept Lydia upright.

"Reach. Now!" Phoebe shouted.

Before she could lift her arm, Jesus turned the corner to the synagogue. The crowd surged, knocking Lydia and Phoebe forward. Lydia did not have the strength to stay afoot as someone assailed her from behind. Her body plunged toward the trampled soil. "No!"

Her chest collided with the path. Air fled from her lungs as her hands struck jagged pebbles. Phoebe's fingers plucked at the back of

Lydia's garment, but her friend's attempts to help were useless. Sandaled feet assaulted Lydia like she was a doormat.

A flash of blue among the sandals caught her attention. Could it be the fringe of the rabbi's robe? The bold color of a *tzitzit*? *Let it be, Lord. For I know if I only touch Your clothes, I shall be healed.*

She thrust her arm into the fray of ankles toward the beacon of blue. Her fingers caressed the threads of a tassel hanging from Jesus's garment. Cotton, with a cool gentleness of silk, brushed her fingertips. "Jesus, heal me." Her plea barely registered amidst the chorus of requests shouted at Jesus.

A bolt of fire traveled through her hand and up her arm, spreading over her entire body. This surge was unlike the heat from the crowd and gentler than the heat from the sun. The fire imitated a pleasant inferno, powerful, yet controlled. Her whole body tingled. *Get up.* Whether Phoebe had commanded her or Elon or her subconscious, she knew not. She needed to rise quickly or risk injury. She pushed herself from the ground.

Phoebe wrapped an arm around Lydia's waist.

A giddiness overcame Lydia's senses as she stood. She had the power to stand among the throng of the crowd. Below her belly, her muscles tightened as if made new. Her legs held her upright with no threat of a fall, or gush of blood. Her curse had vanished. She had been healed by this man, this Messiah, this Jesus. She stared at her fingers, still tingling from the stroke of a tassel. She stifled a shriek of joy. The Lord had heard her cries, and He had halted her bleeding. He had made her whole and clean after twelve years of isolation and misery.

Oh, the glee to tell Phoebe that her support wasn't needed.

The movement of the crowd slowed. Jesus whirled to face the people surrounding Lydia and Phoebe. His gaze searched the faces yearning for His attention.

"Who touched my clothes?" Jesus asked.

Lydia chilled at His question. Had she done something wrong? Cast dishonor on the Messiah? Made Him unclean? Her body began to tremble. If she hurried away, everyone would know she had touched Jesus. Would the crowd chase her down, recognize her, and treat her like a criminal? She had nowhere to hide. *God, help me.*

FOUR

Peter scrubbed a hand through his beard while deflecting the swarm of the crowd with his other arm. A few disciples tried to reason with the people, but no one practiced patience with Jesus being within their grasp.

Had Jesus asked who had touched Him? People reached from everywhere. How would those closest, he, John, or James, know the exact hand that had touched Jesus? Was this a test? If it was, he would fail.

"Who touched me?" Jesus's voice rose as He examined the crowd.

James shrugged. "Master, you see the numbers crowding against us. How can we answer you?"

Peter nodded in agreement. "Everywhere we go you are touched. We may never know who it was."

Jairus shifted his weight side to side. The synagogue ruler uttered a half-hearted blessing to those who pleaded for attention.

Steadfast, Jesus continued his scan of the thickening crowd.

John formed a blockade next to his brother, James. "I agree. We must keep moving. The numbers here are growing rapidly."

Surely, Jesus would heed John's reason. Crowds rarely rattled John's demeanor.

A woman ducked under Peter's arm. Her head covering caught on his elbow, revealing her dark ringlets. She dropped to her knees in front of Jesus with her face almost kissing His toes.

"It was I who touched you." The woman trembled violently as she spoke. "I have been an outcast for twelve years, but today, with barely a touch, You healed my shame."

Would Jesus be satisfied with her confession? Peter raised his arm to protect the woman from onlookers.

Jesus remained idle in the middle of the path. Peter knew that grin on Jesus's face. He had seen it many times. Even though the clamor around Jesus increased, the disciples would remain by his side, giving Him room for a conversation, for Jesus wanted to listen.

Lydia inhaled the clay scent of dirt. Head to the ground, she dared not gaze into the face of the Messiah, or she would weep.

Somehow, in this crowd of people reaching for Him, hoping for a healing, Jesus knew she had touched Him, and that He had healed her. Did everyone who was healed sense His power? Was that why He sought her? Had He felt the warm sensation leave His body and go forth into hers? Was that why He did not keep walking? Jesus had to know that she had been unclean, and He had banished the disease from her body.

"I touched You." Her words stuttered, strangled by her stampeding heartbeat. "I have bled for twelve long years. I tried everything to stop the bleeding. Nothing ceased the flow. I've suffered for so long that I had given up hope. I didn't think God cared about me, but then I heard about You."

Beyond their intimate circle, people called out to Jesus. Closer in, voices hushed others as if they knew Jesus listened to her confession. Was He waiting for an acknowledgement of her healing? How did one thank the Messiah?

Her gaze swept to His face. His eyes glistened like he understood her misery. Like he had been there year after year, consoling her agony.

"When I touched Your clothing, I was healed." Her throat seized. "I could feel the strength of the woman I once was returning to my limbs. A miracle of God was at work in my body. *Toda raba, Adonai.* You heard my cries. My prayers. My plea."

Jesus's eyes shone all the brighter, like they had trapped the sheen from the lake.

"Daughter, your faith has healed you."

Daughter. Her chest seized on the word her own father had forgotten.

"Go in peace and be freed from your suffering."

Gone. Her suffering was all gone. She was free to walk among her people and worship God without blame and banishment.

Jesus eased away and carried on as a runner approached. The man sought the synagogue ruler accompanying Jesus.

In this moment, she didn't bother herself with the concerns of the synagogue. The Messiah was here in Capernaum, and she had touched Him and talked to Him.

Suddenly, she was wrapped in an embrace. Phoebe wept into Lydia's breast. Her friend clutched her tight.

Lydia need not fear becoming faint from Phoebe's embrace, for she was not the frail woman who had hobbled into the crowd. Her skin glowed with health, and she was able to move forthright.

As she and Phoebe made their way toward their cart, Elon emerged from the shade of the terebinth tree. His cheeks were tear-stained, but his smile rivaled the grandeur of the sea.

"You saw?" Lydia asked, elation bubbling inside her chest.

"I saw." His smile grew. "It was all I could do to keep myself from lifting you into Jesus's arms."

"I've been in God's arms every day since the bleeding started. Some days I forgot that truth, and other days it seemed like my prayers were swept far from God. He reminded me that I needed to hold firmly to my thread of belief. The wise counsel of my friend and my betrothed convinced me to seek Jesus."

Elon eased closer. He glanced around before caressing her cheek. "We need to plan a wedding feast."

Phoebe giggled. "And fast. The way you two are looking at one another, this tree is going to be set ablaze."

Elon laughed. Lydia laughed. Such a welcome song. One she would enjoy each new God-given day.

Thanks be to God.

AUTHOR REFLECTIONS

Over the years, I have heard the story of the woman who suffered from bleeding for twelve years. I imagined her standing upright and boldly touching Jesus's cloak to be healed (Mark 5:27). It wasn't until I sat in the basement of a chapel in Magdala, Israel, that I imagined this scene differently. As I sat in the historic basement, on rock benches from the first century, I stared at a mural created by artist Daniel Coriola. The mural, "Encounter," depicted sandaled male feet crowded together. In the midst of the feet was a woman's hand reaching toward the hem of a robe. This image gave me a new understanding about the woman of blood. Maybe she wasn't as healthy as I had previously thought.

In my story, I have Lydia's bleeding beginning with her menstrual cycle. We are not specifically told that is when her bleeding began, but a constant bleeding for twelve years is unlikely from another part of the body. A cycle of bleeding that never ends could be caused by a period. Also, per the Levitical laws (Leviticus 15:19-33), a woman with menstrual bleeding would be unclean and forced to separate from people for seven days. If her bleeding continued, her separation—and isolation—would continue.

Constant bleeding would lead to the possibility of anemia and fatigue. The woman of blood also "suffered a great deal under the care of many doctors" (Mark 5:26). We are told that she grew worse. This

AUTHOR REFLECTIONS

treatment could mean more bleeding, or bloodletting, was performed as was customary in ancient times.

I know what it is like to be anemic. My first pregnancy was a ruptured ectopic pregnancy. An ectopic pregnancy is when the fertilized egg, a baby, travels down the fallopian tube toward the uterus, but doesn't make it to its destination. My baby's journey stopped, and my baby implanted in the fallopian tube. As my baby grew, the tube eventually ruptured, causing internal bleeding. By the time I arrived at the hospital, and the doctors figured out why I was fainting, I was rushed to the operating room. By the end of my surgery, I had lost half of my blood supply.

For better or worse, I did not get a blood transfusion but elected to build my blood volume by resting and eating gourmet meals prepared by my mom. Energy, you ask? I had none. I rose to eat a meal and then slept until the next one. My husband had to help me walk as I was extremely weak. Traveling to a crowded area in the heat of the day would have been impossible for me.

If the woman bleeding for twelve years had lost a substantial amount of blood, she may not have boldly walked toward Jesus. My Lydia is weak and caught in a crowd desperate to see Jesus. The woman might have fallen and only been able to grasp the hem of a cloak. It is a possibility, but we will never know this side of heaven where she actually touched Jesus's cloak. The accounts in Matthew and Luke say that the woman touched "the edge of his cloak."

The Galilee region has a warm climate. Bodies crammed together can cause an increase in temperature as well. One of those bodies may recognize an unclean woman who was forbidden to touch others lest the other person become unclean and in need of ceremonial washing. There are a host of reasons that could have kept this woman from Jesus, but she came to Him anyway.

I have Lydia see a flash of color on a tassel or *tzitzit* worn by Jesus. I included this upon the urging of a Jewish believer, a friend of mine named Tovah. You can find these tassels commanded by God to be worn in Numbers 15:37-41 and Deuteronomy 22:12. The color of the tassel is up for debate, and the dye has been lost over the years. Some scholars say the *tekhelet* color was blue or blue-violet, and others say it had a green hue. We will never truly know for sure.

We do know for certain that this woman believed Jesus could heal her. After all the years of suffering, she had faith in God. Jesus commends her faith, but He doesn't discount her suffering. Jesus mentions her suffering in verse 34, "Daughter, your faith has healed you. Go in peace and be freed from your suffering." At this appointed moment in time, Jesus heals this woman. He intimately knows this woman and uses a term of endearment to acknowledge her. He calls her His daughter. Jesus understands all the heartache she has gone through. God is omniscient, all-knowing, and He knows this woman's history and heart.

For all of us, physical healing isn't enough. Don't get me wrong, if you are in pain, physical healing is wonderful, but Jesus also gives this woman spiritual healing. He gives her eternal life. She can "go in peace" because she sought Jesus and believed He was God.

This poor woman of blood had encountered charlatans intent on taking her money. When she encountered Jesus, she came into the presence of the true healer, the Creator of the universe, her Creator. She believed Jesus was who He said he was, the Son of the Most High God.

I don't know what you are facing today, physically or spiritually. In most parts of the world, women aren't cast out into a tent when they get their period or separated from others if they cut themselves and need a bandage. There are diseases, however, that do isolate people, and isolation can be a depressing and lonely circumstance. Some diseases cause daily pain and hardship. How much more do we need a Comforter and Savior during these times? Some of my favorite verses in times of hardship are Philippians 4:4-7.

I hope this story of the woman of blood touches your heart and has you taking inventory of the time you spend with Jesus. We need Him every day, not just when we are ill. I also hope we can all look at people differently because we need each other, especially when our bodies become sick or weak.

May your faith be as strong as the woman of blood's, who had a faith so vibrant that she ventured into an unforgiving crowd to seek

AUTHOR REFLECTIONS

God incarnate and believed that, with a single touch of a garment, anything was possible.

DISCUSSION QUESTIONS

DISCUSSION ONE

Read the account of the woman bleeding for twelve years in Matthew 9:18-22 and Luke 8:40-48. These accounts are very similar between the Gospels. Is there anything that stands out in these other accounts in relation to the verses in Mark 5:21-34?

_____
_____
_____
_____

DISCUSSION TWO

The story of the woman bleeding for twelve years is intertwined with that of Jairus—the synagogue ruler who sought Jesus to heal his sick daughter. We will study that account next. What does it tell us about Jesus that He was able to converse with and show compassion to a hurting woman while the synagogue ruler waited?

Read Psalm 103 and note what stands out about God's compassion for His people.

DISCUSSION QUESTIONS

_____
_____
_____

DISCUSSION THREE

Look up *compassion* and *sympathy* in a dictionary. What nouns and verbs are associated with these words?

_____
_____
_____
_____

We live in a hurting world. Take a moment to think of your family, friends, people at church, work, or even a neighbor. Is there someone you could encourage?

_____
_____
_____
_____

The woman of blood suffered for twelve years. I give Lydia a servant to keep her company in my story, but we don't know if the woman of blood had an attendant. The laws of cleanliness would be a burden in biblical times.

Think of a concrete way you can show love to someone who is hurting or lonely, whether it's through a text, phone call, card, or some other gift. What concrete need did Elon take care of for Lydia?

_____
_____
_____
_____

DISCUSSION QUESTIONS

I have heard it said that we have time, treasure, and talents. Use one of those to bring happiness into someone's life this week.

Note: If you are doing this Bible study with a group, share how you showed encouragement to someone at your next meeting.

DISCUSSION FOUR

In Mark 5:30, we are told that Jesus realized power had gone out from Him. We know that power went into the bleeding woman and healed her. What do you think this transfer felt like? What would your reaction be to this miracle?

How would it change your life to be healed and "freed from suffering" instantly? (Mark 5:29)

_____
_____
_____
_____

The only mention in the Gospels (Matthew, Mark, Luke, and John) of Jesus calling someone "daughter" occurs in this story. What impact would that word have had on a woman isolated for twelve years?

_____
_____
_____
_____

DISCUSSION FIVE

In the twenty-first century, we have all sixty-six books of the Bible. There are several translations of the Bible with study guides and notes, and they are widely available online and at physical stores. We look back in time to Jesus's Galilee ministry when Jesus prepared to give His life for our sins and conquer death. We have eye-witness accounts of the resurrection, and those who trust in Jesus have the indwelling of the Holy Spirit (Acts 2:38-39, John 14:25-26).

The woman of blood met Jesus during his public ministry, pre-crucifixion. Through her illness, she stayed faithful to God. Where do you think her strength and faith came from? Read Genesis 12:1-9 and Deuteronomy chapter 6 to find out about the Covenant that God made with His people. Share the verses that have special meaning to you and most likely inspired an outcast to seek Jesus.

_____
_____
_____
_____

Do you come from a family of faith in Jesus or are you a new believer? How has your faith journey impacted your life? If you are a new believer in Christ, how do you hope your relationship with Jesus changes your life?

_____
_____
_____
_____

DISCUSSION SIX

Walking around the Sea of Galilee where Jesus walked was a humbling experience. Isaiah prophesied about this area (Isaiah 9:1-2), and Matthew quotes the following prophecy when Jesus fulfills it.

Matthew 4:12-17

When Jesus heard that John had been put in prison, he returned to Galilee. Leaving Nazareth, he went and lived in Capernaum, which was by the lake in the area of Zebulun and Naphtali—to fulfill what was said through the prophet Isaiah:

> *"Land of Zebulun and land of Naphtali. The way to the sea, along the Jordan, Galilee of the Gentiles—*
>
> *The people living in darkness have seen a great light; on those living in the land of the shadow of death a light has dawned."*
>
> *From that time on Jesus began to preach, "Repent for the kingdom of heaven is near."*

The woman of blood emerged from the shadow of death and met the light of the world—Jesus. We can meet Jesus every minute of every day when He is our Savior and Lord. We can rejoice and receive that special name of "daughter" or "son" given by Jesus. Spend some time this week praying and abiding with the light of the world.

Part THREE
Fashionably Late

Scripture Passage:
Mark 5:21-24; 5:35-43

ONE

While Jesus was still speaking, some men came from the house of Jairus, the synagogue ruler. "Your daughter is dead," they said.
"Why bother the teacher anymore?"
Mark 5:35

Jairus gripped the back of his neck and squeezed the skin until a pinch of pain traveled down his spine. The sun had warmed the skin below the coils of his turban, but the blazing heat inside his chest threatened to consume him.

Hadn't the people on the shore heard his request? Surely those closest to Jesus recalled the earnestness in his plea for Jesus to heal his daughter. His precious little girl was dying. And yet, the crowd seemed callous to his urgent need. They begged for Jesus to heal ailments that did not lead to death. His daughter had only seen twelve years. If Jesus did not lay hands on her and heal her, Jairus feared she may not last until sunset. In his heart, he believed Jesus could bring back his daughter's inquisitive smile. Remembering her gaunt, lifeless features as she rested in bed almost caused him to wail.

He crossed his arms over his chest and rocked back and forth, hoping the movement spurred Jesus to continue down the road. His insides churned with each passing minute.

A woman had collapsed at Jesus's feet. Jairus did not recognize her. Most people respected his position at the synagogue and would defer to his standing since his child ailed. Who would remain loyal and take up his cause, urging Jesus to hurry? Sadly, no one pled for Jesus to follow him, even though he had allowed Jesus room at the synagogue to instruct the people of Capernaum.

Jairus tried to catch Peter's attention. The fisherman had been shouting for the crowd to stop pressing the teacher. When he snagged a brief glance from the burly fisherman, Jairus shook his hands in the air. If he wasn't careful, he might strike a neighbor. He did not care. He could not care. His daughter struggled to catch her next breath.

Peter acknowledged him with a tip of his head.

At last, the woman rose, spoke briefly, and burrowed into the crowd.

Jairus regained his position at Jesus's side. He clutched a hand to his chest and breathed in the stifling, humid air.

The main road was bordered on one side by homes with courtyards filled with curious onlookers. A market of millstones stood like a wall on the other side of the thoroughfare. Masses clogged the road, leaving little space for a hurried escape. Could the people not see his desperation soaring by the moment?

Jesus traveled with him, away from the sea, and toward the houses near the synagogue. Finally, they were making progress.

"Jairus." His brother waved his arm and shouldered past people blocking his path.

Jairus's stomach clenched. With the intensity of his brother's charge, Jairus feared his words would not bring a greeting or a good report. A synagogue elder trailed after his brother, his face downcast.

"Your daughter is dead," his brother rasped. A tear leaked from his eye. "She is gone." He glanced at Jesus and the commotion all around. "Why bother the teacher any more?"

Jairus closed his eyes and focused on the amber circle illuminating the blackness of his eyelids. He had to remain strong and not collapse in the dirt. A crowd watched his every move. With every ounce of fortitude he had left, he uttered his plea anew. "My daughter is not a bother. She needs to see Jesus."

TWO

Jairus opened his eyes. How many in the crowd had heard his brother's announcement? Not many, for where was their outcry? A roar of agony threatened to rush from his lips. Was his little girl truly no more? It couldn't be. His chest heaved.

"Come with us." His brother motioned in the direction of Jairus's house. The home where the corpse of his daughter rested. "Your wife has need of you."

What of his own need? Should he show his despair to those who had heard him speak of God's favor and provision? How many times had he commanded his people to pray and petition God for answers? He did not like this answer. He had to believe that Jesus could heal even death, for if Jesus failed him, Jairus would question God's wisdom, without anger, but with a damaged heart.

The press of a sure and steady hand weighed upon his shoulder. Fingers kneaded his tight muscles. Jesus stood in front of Jairus, blocking the muttering inquisition of those nearby. No grief creased Jesus's features. The heat of the day cast a glow on His skin as His eyes squinted from the brightness.

"Don't be afraid," Jesus beseeched him. "Just believe."

If Jairus had not watched the words formed by Jesus's lips and felt the brush of His breath, he would have thought someone had misrepresented the teacher's meaning. Jesus said to believe. Believe in a transformation from death to life. He had heard that Jesus performed healings from leprosy and fevers, but he had not heard of a revival of the soul. Who, but God, could restore life? His mind whirled with Jesus's promise, but the image of his daughter's frail form lying in the middle of mourners made him almost swoon.

Jesus stepped back and spoke to His closest followers, the ones always by his side.

Can I believe in life? From death? For my little girl?

Jairus lifted his hands toward the cloudless sky. *Help me believe, God Almighty. I have nothing to offer You or my daughter. I want so much to believe Jesus. To see my daughter well. Banish any unbelief.*

His brother fidgeted. "We must go."

"We will wait for Jesus." Saying those words, audibly and with fervor, strengthened his conviction. "I am following Him."

Peter jogged to catch Jesus and the sons of Zebedee, James and John. The other disciples were left to satisfy the mass of people. Mutterings in the crowd relayed the announcement of the death of the synagogue ruler's daughter. Few people rushed after their small group. Stragglers stayed at a respectful distance. Were they taking pity on Jairus and giving him room to grieve? They were wise to avoid insulting the religious leader with their insensitivity. Andrew, Matthew, and the others organized the fray that beckoned for healing.

John gave him a side-eye look and lifted his brows. He cocked his head toward the crowd of people congregating near the main road and the synagogue.

"Did the man say Jairus's daughter had died?"

John had ears to listen the same as he did. From all accounts, the girl had succumbed to an illness. What Jesus planned to do about it now was anybody's guess.

Jesus maintained a brisk pace and did not carry on a conversation. Was He summoning the words to console Jairus's wife and family?

Peter leaned closer to John. "I pray they were misinformed. If not, this could be a trap to claim Jesus is a false teacher. We could lose the support of the synagogue ruler."

"Don't both those roads lead to the same marketplace?"

Clapping a hand on John's shoulder, Peter said, "I am learning as much."

The distant din of wailing drew Peter's attention to two large homes joined by a substantial courtyard. Ahead, a group of women in dark-colored cloaks cried loudly and openly in front of the farthest home. A small crowd had already gathered. Screams of distress penetrated the breeze.

Peter stiffened. The girl's death was not a lie.

The synagogue ruler wept when observing the mourners.

If this was a scheme concocted by the religious elites, Jesus strode toward it with confidence. His countenance never faltered.

Jesus continued past the women who beat their breasts as cries echoed forth. More subdued mourners parted as Jesus, Jairus, and Jairus's brother entered the home.

Peter shuffled in a procession after John and James. The incense burning in the home cast a haze in the front room. His nose itched, but he did not complain. Jairus's wife, clothed in a plain dress and veil, sobbed in a chair stationed at the back of the living area near a doorway. Hands covering her face, she did not acknowledge her husband or Jesus. Jairus hurried to her side.

Jesus stopped in the middle of the room and held up his arms. "Why all this commotion and wailing? The child is not dead but asleep."

Stunned family members glared; their faces wrinkled with contempt. A shriek startled Peter as Jairus's wife collapsed onto the floor.

John stepped next to Peter. "Clear the room except for Jairus and his wife. You and James can stay as well. Be kind but do it swiftly."

Peter could act swiftly. The kind and compassionate part he would have to work on. He didn't take well to relatives scoffing at his Teacher, the Son of God.

THREE

Jairus supported his wife with one arm and moved her toward the bedroom. Her eyes glistened as she searched his face for the reason he returned her to the bedroom tomb.

"Where are we going?"

He had no truth for her, only a wisp of hope. His wife glanced at some neighbors who loudly contested their forced departure.

"Jesus wants to see our daughter. That is all. Do not worry. The others can come back later." For what, he had no idea, but Jesus was finally here in his home, and Jairus would do whatever the teacher asked. His gut had told him many times that Jesus was no ordinary rabbi, for He knew the Law better than those schooled since childhood. The people responded to Jesus's teaching, and to His healing touch. From His touch came miracles not explained by educated men. Or by priests who pronounced the sick to be clean.

"Come along." Jairus escorted his wife into the bedroom. Jesus followed with three of his friends.

Jairus nearly collapsed upon observing his daughter's prone form in the bed. No greeting, not even a twitch, greeted him. Her eyelids were bathed in gray, and her lips matched the purple of a grape. The rosy color of her cheeks that turned her smile into a blessing had fled.

He stifled a well of tears, but one slid down his nose and plunged to the floor.

Jesus knelt by the bed and leaned forward as if to tell his little girl a tale of His travels. He took her hand and held it between His. The width of His palms hid the stiffness in Jairus's daughter's fingers.

My baby girl. Jairus quietly released a sob. His wife rested her head on his chest. He drew her closer, unsure of what more this day would bring, or if he could stay upright one more minute.

"*Talitha koum!*"

Little girl, I say to you, get up!

Jesus said the command as if He were coaxing a child to come and play.

Jairus's heartbeat exploded in his ears. What was the teacher doing? His daughter was dead, not ill. She could not move. Was this a test of a ruler's faith?

His daughter's eyes opened.

"Our girl is alive!" Jairus's knees nearly buckled. He managed to remain on his feet by bracing a hand on the wall.

His wife gasped. "My baby."

Eyes bright, his daughter smiled at Jesus. That familiar smile caused Jairus to suppress an exuberant cry. He could barely utter a syllable of praise.

Before he knew what was happening, his daughter sat, shifted to the edge of the bed, and stood. She rushed toward him and his wife and wrapped her arms around them. Tilting her head backward, she grinned into their faces.

His mind couldn't conceive what he had witnessed. God was here, in a bedroom, restoring his family. More tears flooded his face.

"I did not see you before I fell asleep, *Abba.*" His daughter's embrace grew warm and snug.

Jairus removed his arm from his wife's shoulder and knelt before his daughter. His tears became a raging river.

"I was here. I went to get to Jesus. I wanted Him to meet you and to make you feel better." He squeezed her into a hug. "I love you, my girl."

His wife joined the intimate reunion.

Jesus came alongside the huddle of Jairus's small family. The deep rumble of Jesus's voice mixing with his little girl's chatter swept his mind into a whirlwind. Jesus spoke, but Jairus was struck dumb. What did one say after such a miracle?

This rabbi had brought a dead daughter back to life before his eyes. She had died, but now she lived. This guest was no ordinary teacher or healer. No mere man brought people out of the grave. Could it be? Was it true? Was Jesus the Messiah? Surely, this man was sent by God.

Jairus offered his eternal gratefulness.

Jesus smiled and strode toward the door. He conversed with two of his friends. Their faces mirrored the awe streaking through Jairus's veins. When Jesus had finished talking, He left the room.

"If you didn't catch that," the burly friend of Jesus said, rubbing his bearded chin, "He desires that you do not speak about this. And ..." Peter glanced at Jairus's little girl, who twirled in circles at his side. "You should give your daughter something to eat."

The man's, Peter's, stomach growled. He laughed, some color returning to his cheeks. "That is the only predictable event that has happened today."

AUTHOR REFLECTIONS

When you visit Capernaum, you have no doubt this town on the Sea of Galilee was Jesus's home base for His public ministry. As you enter the ruins, a huge sign states "Capharnaum. Home of Jesus." I shouldn't have been surprised that Jesus resided here, for Scripture tells us this fact in Matthew 4:13-16 (NIV), which is a reference to Isaiah 9:1-2. We looked at these verses in our last lesson.

I had heard Jesus referred to as "Jesus of Nazareth" because He grew up in Nazareth, but I had never heard Jesus called "Jesus of Capernaum." Both towns border the Sea of Galilee.

As I walked along the central pathway through Capernaum, I was stunned that Peter lived in Capernaum. The ruins of the fisherman's house are near the Sea of Galilee. He didn't have a long walk to work. Had Jesus slept and stayed at Peter's house? More than likely He did, and He would have had easy access to fishing boats to cross the lake.

Trees line the main swath through Capernaum. Were they there in Jesus's day? We do not know. I have Lydia and Elon reuniting under a terebinth tree.

Archaeologists have unearthed a myriad of millstones near the location of Peter's house. The stones are huge and heavy. I wouldn't like to try to lift one. I had a better understanding of the references to a millstone being placed around your neck after seeing the large stones.

AUTHOR REFLECTIONS

Jesus mentions millstones in Matthew 18:6 and Mark 9:42.

And if anyone causes one of these little ones who believe in me to sin, it would be better for him to be thrown into the sea with a large millstone tied around his neck. Mark 9:42 (NIV)

Were the millstones located in Capernaum when Jesus stayed with Peter? Again, we do not know. I make the stones a hindrance to poor Jairus and the crowds.

The story of Jairus and the bleeding woman both include the number twelve. In the story of Jairus, his daughter is twelve years old. Is there a significance in both stories, including the number? We will have to ask Jesus in heaven, as scholars haven't decided if there is any meaning attached to the number in these accounts.

Jairus is mentioned as a synagogue ruler in Mark 5:22, 35, 36, and 38. Not many details are known about the duties of a synagogue ruler in Jesus's day. Sources seem to believe the rulers were similar to the modern-day office of deacons, who take care of the practical duties of building maintenance and keeping a church facility ready for worship. Synagogue rulers more than likely supervised the worship, prayers, and teaching that occurred in the synagogue. With these responsibilities came respect and standing in the community. Jairus does not seem hesitant about seeking Jesus. He fell at Jesus's feet among a crowd of people who worshiped at the synagogue. Jairus's actions make it seem that he truly believed Jesus had the power to heal his daughter.

I visited the ruins of a synagogue in Capernaum. The building is not the same synagogue mentioned in Mark, but the building was constructed on top of a first-century structure. Could it be the original synagogue? We don't know. I placed the synagogue in my story in a similar location to the one I visited. The synagogue is close to Peter's house, but it's farther down the main road, away from the water.

Being in Capernaum and seeing the archaeological ruins gave me a better understanding of the logistics of Jesus's ministry. I am still in awe at the miracles Jesus performed and the compassion He showed to the sick and hurting. Jesus is still showing compassion to the sick and hurting today. Jesus loved us so much that He laid down His life for us.

AUTHOR REFLECTIONS

The woman bleeding for twelve years and the synagogue ruler left their homes to seek Jesus. Their faith guided them to the Son of God. May we always seek God, no matter what we are going through in our lives.

Jesus told Jairus and his wife and daughter not to speak about the miracle. Jesus was on a timetable only He knew. He doesn't give us the instruction to stay quiet about His miracles. He gives us the opposite command in the Great Commission found in Matthew 28:18-20. May we always find time to share about our faith in Jesus and to tell people about our compassionate Savior.

DISCUSSION QUESTIONS

Read the other accounts about Jairus in Matthew 9:18-25, and Luke 8:40-53.

DISCUSSION ONE

Jairus is not only a synagogue ruler in Capernaum, he is also a parent. My heart goes out to him in Mark 5:22-23 when he falls at Jesus's feet and pleads for Him to heal his daughter.

Given his position, do you think this public expression of humility came easily to Jairus? What would you have done in his situation?

_____
_____
_____
_____

DISCUSSION TWO

In the gospel of Mark, Jairus receives the news about his daughter's death while Jesus is searching for—and talking to—the woman

DISCUSSION QUESTIONS

bleeding for twelve years. How do you think Jairus felt about this delay?

_____
_____
_____
_____

After Jairus receives the terrible news of his daughter's death, Jesus tells him in Mark 5:36, "Don't be afraid; just believe."

Would these words comfort you, or would you still be in a state of panic?

_____
_____
_____
_____

DISCUSSION THREE

In Matthew's account of the healing of Jairus's daughter, Jairus tells Jesus that his daughter has died (Matthew 9:18). What does this tell us about Jairus's faith?

_____
_____
_____
_____

Even though the timing of the announcement of the death of Jairus's daughter varies between the Gospels, the outcome of the story is the same. A dead girl is brought back to life by the Giver of Life. Matthew has a condensed style of relaying the story compared to the other Gospel writers.

Do we get any clues to the extent of Jairus's faith in the Bible passages relating to his daughter's miracle? If so, what stands out to you?

DISCUSSION FOUR

Mark is the only writer to record Jesus's words in the first century Aramaic language. *Talitha koum!* translated is "Little girl, I say to you, get up!" Scholars say Aramaic is probably the language Jesus and His followers used most often.

Did the girl wait to rise? No, she's out of that bed immediately, standing and walking.

What would your reaction be as a parent? Or as a curious resident of Capernaum?

How does Jesus show his human side in what he tells the girl's parents to do for her?

DISCUSSION FIVE

When I originally drafted my fictional story, I gave the little girl a

DISCUSSION QUESTIONS

name. Afterward, I took out the name and left references to her as "little girl" or "daughter." The girl is not given a name in the Bible.

Does this make a difference to the account? Would you have read my story differently if I had called the girl Rebekah, Martha, Junia, etc.?

_____
_____
_____
_____

DISCUSSION SIX

In Luke 12:6-7, Jesus speaks to His disciples and tells them, *"Are not five sparrows sold for two pennies? Yet not one of them is forgotten by God. Indeed, the very hairs of your head are numbered. Don't be afraid; you are worth more than many sparrows."*

I hope you feel loved, especially loved by God. He created you in His image and crafted you into a unique and special person.

Make a list of all that God has done for you this week, or even this very day. Next time you see a bird, remember how much you are loved by God.

_____
_____
_____
_____

In the last two stories, we have seen Jesus engage with a suffering woman and resurrect a young girl. Jesus shows compassion to the young, the old, and those in between.

For God so loved the world that he gave his one and only Son, that whoever believes in him shall not perish but have eternal life.
John 3:16

DISCUSSION QUESTIONS

Find a verse in the Bible about Jesus's love and share it with your group or write it below as a reminder of His love.

_____

_____

_____

_____

Part FOUR
Not Even a Pillow

Scripture Passage:
Mark 6:1-13

ONE

Calling the Twelve to him, he sent them out two by two and gave them authority over evil spirits.
Mark 6:7

Peter leaned against the stone wall of the synagogue in the nearby town of Nazareth. His back muscles tightened as the uncustomary din of conversations competed with Jesus's teaching. Where was the respect and acceptance due a neighbor's son? The crowds in the synagogue at Capernaum had remained reverent throughout the reading and discussion of God's Word. Jairus did not tolerate talking during the Sabbath worship. This noise while Jesus preached was unacceptable. Peter took a deep breath to cool his indignation. If he had a bucket of water, he would douse these chattering fools.

The synagogue ruler in Nazareth wormed his way through the rows of men without a care to his disruption of Jesus's instruction. On the other side of the building's entrance, the gazes of Peter's fellow disciples followed the path of the rude synagogue official. Did John and James share Peter's disbelief at this insult?

A finely dressed man spoke briefly with the official and hurried toward the entrance of the synagogue. The man secured his sash as he strode toward the door. He squinted at Peter, assessing him with a scowl.

"Are you with the carpenter?"

Peter stepped from the back wall and accompanied the man into the warmth of the Saturday morning sun. The man questioned him too loudly for an answer inside the synagogue. Peter guided the nobleman into the shade of an olive tree. The man did not protest. Did he expect an answer because of his station, or did curiosity hold his attention?

"We came from Capernaum two days ago." Peter forced a host's smile, even though he bristled at the man's lack of propriety. "Jesus has been staying with me. I have a home by the lake."

"Capernaum? What's he doing there? His brothers live around Nazareth. At least James and Joseph do. I saw his sisters earlier." The shade had not cooled this man's ire. Why couldn't he worship God and not cast doubt upon Jesus's authority?

Peter shuffled his sandals. He couldn't leave Nazareth fast enough.

"I am a fisherman. In my boats, I can take Jesus all over Galilee so He can teach about the kingdom of God."

The man glanced at Peter's hands.

Peter clasped them to hide the calluses from his labor.

"Jesus is not a rabbi. He's Mary's son. He works with his hands the same as you." The nobleman shook his head. The turban securing his graying hair did not move. "It isn't right for him to teach in our synagogue. His family should have put a stop to it." The man ambled out of the shade. "Take him back to Capernaum." He strode south with his head swaying back and forth, registering his disdain.

Peter grabbed a branch above him, watched the man's retreat, and waited. Waited for his heart rhythm to return to normal. Rage on the Sabbath was a sin.

He didn't know how long he lingered under the olive tree, but it was long enough for Jesus to join him in the shade, along with the other disciples.

"Only in his hometown, among his relatives and in his own house is a prophet without honor," Jesus said to them.

He cast a knowing look at Peter as if He had somehow heard the nobleman's insults.

Summoning a light-hearted tone, Peter asked, "When are we going back to my house in Capernaum?"

TWO

Home. Peter relaxed beside the low-burning fire warming his courtyard. His wife had outdone herself preparing mutton stew and dipping bread. A slight aroma of leeks hung in the smoky air, reminding his stomach of the satisfying meal. His fellow disciples reclined around the firepit and chatted about the journey from Nazareth. They had accompanied Jesus from village to village as He taught about the kingdom of God. Some listeners repented of their wrongdoing and believed in Jesus while other hearts remained as unmoved as the packed dirt on the merchant roads they trod.

Jesus rose and stood near the coals of cedarwood glowing in the pit. The bright orange hue did not illuminate a grin or a contented smile. The man who banished storms and terrified demons appeared weary. Peter moved closer to his Lord, resting near Jesus's feet.

Jesus cleared his throat. The chatter in the courtyard quieted. Only a few pops from the cedar disturbed the night air.

"It is time I sent you to the lost sheep of Israel. They need to hear that the kingdom of heaven is near."

Peter sat straighter. Were the disciples to go without Jesus? How many would heed a fisherman's teaching?

"Take nothing for the journey except a staff—no bread, no bag, no money in your belts." Jesus surveyed the circle of men intent on his instructions.

"Who travels without money?" Judas whispered behind Peter.

Peter wasn't concerned about a lack of coins in his pouch, but not having a bag for necessities, or a waterskin, was unheard of in the desert. He glanced at his brother, whose harvest-moon eyes beheld Jesus.

Jesus stepped to his right and paced near the opening to the courtyard. Lamplight from inside the home backlit his frame.

"Wear sandals but not an extra tunic. Whenever you enter a house, stay there until you leave that town."

"Lodging for two?" James asked.

Working men understood the burden the accommodations might place on a host. A carpenter's son understood the burdens of a host as well.

Jesus nodded. "And if any place will not welcome you or listen to you, shake the dust off your feet when you leave as a testimony against them."

The features of the nobleman in Nazareth flashed in Peter's mind as questions rang out in the courtyard.

Matthew elbowed Peter's side. "Are you going with your brother?"

Peter turned and met the former tax collector's grim face. His friend's previous position made him an outcast in several towns. "I believe we would make a fine pair. You know those in power in Tiberias, and I know those in a fishing village not far from Herod's roost."

"This is true." Matthew tipped his head toward Jesus, who conversed with John. "But we are to go to the lost sheep of Israel. Not to the wolves."

Peter stood and fixed his gaze upon his hesitant traveling partner. "Ah, but if we find the wolves, we will find the lost sheep."

THREE

On the shores of a fishing village north of Tiberias, Peter slapped Andrew on the back and bid his brother farewell. James and Andrew were to sail to Tabgha, farther north on the lake. Matthew gripped the bow of the fishing boat and said a prayer over everyone's journey. Without his ornate bag and thick outer tunic, Matthew resembled the men gutting fish on the shore and hurling insults about the day's catch.

Peter breathed in the odor of raw tilapia as hungry gulls squawked overhead. He scanned the shoreline for bearing. Men emptied nets while others repaired damaged ropes. He missed the daily routine of fishing. Fish didn't speak out of turn or beg for healing. These days, he had replaced most of the calluses on his hands with calluses on his feet.

He and Matthew wandered from the lake.

Peter assessed the distant town. Women carried baskets on their heads and hurried toward a crowded street. An elderly man herded goats near a station of acacia trees not far from the bustling road.

"Have you come to steal my catch, Simon?" The boisterous question rumbled in Peter's ear as a heavy hand grasped his shoulder.

Peter turned, curious about the man who knew his given name.

"Ezekiel." The broad sailor with missing front teeth had been a constant presence on the sands of Capernaum years ago. "Your father is not working you hard enough, my friend." Peter returned his friend's stiff-arm embrace and gestured toward the shore. "There aren't enough fish in your net to fill a child's basket."

"Yet I wager I've caught more than you." Ezekiel's tease enlivened his face. "Where is your boat?"

Peter hesitated. He cast a glance at Matthew, who waited nearby, close enough to hear his reply. Peter's mouth parched as he formed the words he had heard Jesus speak many times.

"I did not come to catch fish. I am here to fish for men." He cleared his throat. A few of Ezekiel's workmen gathered behind their boss. Peter hoped the invisible net he was about to cast would overflow with souls. *Be bold.* "I follow Jesus of Nazareth. I have heard Him teach, and I have seen miracles performed before my eyes. I believe He is the Messiah."

"Shh." Ezekiel whirled and waved his workers toward the boats. Returning his attention to Peter, he said, "You cannot speak of Jesus here. Our ruler has loyal followers everywhere. I could throw a stone and hit his palace." He shuffled backward, severing any bond or allegiance.

Peter's stomach hollowed as this good man retreated from the truth. How much more dread would consume his belly if he taught in his hometown and stood rejected among relatives as Jesus had been rejected in Nazareth?

"Herod Antipas's kingdom will end, but the kingdom of God lives on forever." Peter's voice rose as he spoke the words Jesus had taught him. Words he knew in his heart were true. "God's kingdom is near, my friend."

"Don't speak to me of kingdoms." Ezekiel's brow furrowed as he jerked to scan their surroundings. "Not if you want to keep your head. I prefer to keep mine." He trudged toward the shore, barking orders at his men. No farewell rang out to an old friend.

"Jesus is the Son of God," Peter shouted the proclamation.

A man mending nets stared at him. When Peter acknowledged his interest, the man recoiled and continued his task.

Matthew strolled closer. He rubbed his arm as if they had been the ones lugging nets full of fish. "I would shake the dust from my sandals, but we've only taken a few steps."

FOUR

Matthew attempted to finger the coins in his belt bag, but his fingertips grazed only the cloth of his tunic. The scrape of coin upon coin would not calm his unease today. He had never traveled this light on provisions or walked with a sense of being half-dressed.

He and Peter traipsed toward an incline leading to the center of the small fishing village. Peter hadn't spoken since Ezekiel had rejected his plea to follow Jesus. Though Peter always had words ready to fill time and air, this day held a rare silence.

Matthew's palms dampened as they approached the main road through town. Was it his turn to speak of repentance and voice the call to believe in Jesus? If he was recognized, his fellow Jews could scorn his sin of gathering excess taxes to engorge Herod's accounts. His forehead pounded with every footfall.

He stabbed at the hardened dirt with his staff as they approached the end of a few merchant stands. Not far from the last bin of fruit, a cluster of women stirred large stone pots in an open field. With each sweep of their arms, a stale grass scent wafted onto the breeze. Blue- and yellow-colored cloth dried on a line farther up the hillside. A man stood watch over the women. Was he a relative? A Roman overseer? A craftsman?

Near an outcropping of rocks, a young boy huddled over a board covering his lap. The young one's tongue swept over his top lip as he dipped a brush in a bowl balanced on his makeshift bench. Matthew rubbed his own lip. How many times had his father beseeched him to practice sums? Dutifully he figured amounts with his swaying tongue keeping him focused. The habit stopped when his father ridiculed his cracked lips.

Surely, they shouldn't pass this crowd that God had placed before them without proclaiming the news about Jesus. He squeezed his staff and prepared a greeting with a summation of Jesus's words.

As they traveled closer to the overseer, the man crossed in front of the women busily at work. He paced and muttered, but nothing made any sense. Was the man troubled?

Peter swung his arms wide. "We come in the name of Jesus."

Why was Peter always the first to speak? His friend's proclamation caused the women to still and stare.

"Jesus is the Son of the Most High God." Peter lifted his hands to the sky.

Without warning, the pacing man charged Peter.

Matthew lunged to block the intruder. He held his staff horizontally, as if latching a door. The man, face contorted, rammed into the thick middle of the wood. Spittle foamed on his lips as he babbled nonsense.

"Be gone, you spirit of evil," Matthew shouted. He struggled against the overseer's assault. "Leave this place and this man. I command you in the name of Jesus the Christ."

The man fell backward, leaving the wooden staff almost weightless in Matthew's hands. The possessed man's body did not twitch. His eyes remained open, reflecting the brightness of the cloudless sky.

"My husband," a woman shrieked.

One of the women whose vat sat nearest to the man rushed to his side.

Matthew and Peter knelt beside him.

His chest rose and fell. He wasn't dead. Praise be to God.

"Obadiah, wake up." The woman patted her husband's cheek. "Please speak to me." Her words hitched as she rocked with his head cradled in her arms. "What have you done to him?" Tears stained her cheeks.

"We've done nothing to him except release a demon." Matthew eyed the other women shuffling closer. Merchants gathered in front of their booths. Would there be a riot?

"Give him something to eat." Peter stood. "He is alive and well. Too well after attacking a rich man's son." Peter motioned for Matthew to stand. "Your husband is alive because of the power of Jesus, our Messiah. He has power over the evil one. Repent and believe in the Savior who has restored your husband, and all will go well with you."

So much for preparing a testimony. Peter had explained everything to the crowd, and now his companion strolled toward homes scattered over the hillside.

"*Toda raba.*" The woman hiccupped her thanks. "I saw something was wrong, but I didn't know what to do." Her husband stirred. "Thanks be to God. My husband is alive." She stroked the side of his face. "Now, he is free of the evil spirit."

"Offer him some bread for sustenance." Matthew remembered Jesus's instruction. He nodded and acknowledged the gathering of women. "Praise be to the power of the One True God." His spirit emboldened at his words of assurance.

He hurried to catch Peter.

"Wa-it." The summons had a rattled *T* sound.

The boy who had perched near the women raced after him.

"You-you-you saved Ob-di-ah."

Matthew's heart ached at the struggles this young man had with his speech.

"No, I did not save your friend." He knelt to see the boy's face. "Jesus of Nazareth saved your friend. Jesus is the Messiah, the Son of God. You must believe that He is God." Finally, he had a chance to testify about Jesus. His whole being overflowed with joy.

"I-I w-want t-to." The young man bounced on tiptoes, grasping something in his fist.

"What do you have there?" Peter asked.

Couldn't Peter keep quiet for once?

The young man opened his fist. A small, bright yellow wooden fish lay in his palm. A small hook was embedded in the wood. The boy's jaw gaped, and his lips trembled, but no words came forth. Matthew reached out his hand and stroked the boy's jawline. "That is a mighty fine lure. If you want to believe in Jesus, simply believe. God is here, and He is waiting for you."

The young one smiled. "I believe. I heard what you said, and I can't wait to tell my *saba*. He used to be a scribe. My grandfather knows God's law. I want you to meet him." The boy stilled. His eyes grew so big, Matthew thought they might roll down the hill. "You cured my words."

"Oh no, not I but—"

"Jesus cured me," the boy exclaimed.

"You catch on fast, young man." Peter laughed and continued up the path.

Matthew rose, bursting with enough energy to sprint several hillsides. He slowed his steps to encourage the boy's journey. Wait until Jesus heard this story. Matthew stifled a laugh. Jesus probably already knew this story. The Son of God could relate to casting out demons and to healing the ailments of men, even boys.

"Do you have a place to stay tonight?" A hitch never entered the boy's words. "My *saba* will have many questions for you."

"Well, my friend." Matthew grinned as wide as the sea. "I believe we are staying with you and your grandfather. And we are ready to answer all of your questions."

AUTHOR REFLECTIONS

Traveling around the Sea of Galilee in a bus is a lot different from walking the terrain. The landscape around the Sea of Galilee is mountainous, or as I like to call it, *moundy*. We traveled dirt paths that were packed hard and full of rocks. In preparation for our trip to Israel, my husband and I made sure we could walk five miles a day. This was a prerequisite for our tour to make the most of our travel.

After visiting the stunning remnants of the city of Megiddo, where we hiked the incline to the city and strolled around the ruins, an air-conditioned bus waited to take us to our next stop. We even had hotel reservations for each night of our itinerary. When Jesus sent out the Twelve to preach repentance to the lost sheep of Israel, no air-conditioned bus awaited these men after their daily marathon. The disciples had to rely on the hospitality of strangers for their meals and lodging.

When Jesus and His disciples traveled to His hometown of Nazareth, we see that hospitality was in short supply. The arms-length welcome of Jesus may have been on the minds of the disciples as they set out to journey around Galilee.

In my fictional story, I send Peter and Matthew to a fishing town similar to where we stayed in Magdala. Our hotel in Magdala was

AUTHOR REFLECTIONS

built over the biblical ruins of the city. Imagine how thrilled I was to find an archaeological dig occurring in the lobby behind a glass enclosure.

The synagogue discovered in Magdala has a floor decorated with mosaic tiles that were dyed in rich colors. A stone in the synagogue displays carved images from the temple in Jerusalem. Perhaps Magdala was a town brimming with artists?

Archaeologists have unearthed large stone vats, like big pots, in Magdala. Were these used to hold dyes or fish or both? We don't know, but I incorporated dye-making into my story.

Magdala is also located just north of Tiberias, where Herod Antipas lived. Herod Antipas was the son of Herod the Great and ruled over the area of Galilee. Herod Antipas orchestrated the death of John the Baptist, which comes up later in the Gospel of Mark, chapter 6.

My photos of Magdala are picturesque with blue waters and peaceful shores. We know a spiritual battle raged in Magdala. Jesus gave His disciples the ability to cast out demons, and we see Jesus expel demons in the book of Mark. Jesus cast demons from Mary Magdalene, a woman who is surmised to have come from Magdala, and who became an ardent follower of Jesus. (Mark 16:9, Luke 8:1-2)

This portion of Scripture is also full of emotion for Jesus. His homecoming in Nazareth was met with disappointment. Jesus sends His followers on an excursion, leaving Himself without their companionship and words of encouragement. Jesus also hears about the death of his cousin John the Baptist.

I don't know what you are going through in your life. You may feel as if you are traveling over rocky ground without the comforts of a hotel waiting to give you rest. Jesus has traveled the harsh roads you are experiencing, and He promises to be with you every step of the way.

During life's trials, I claim these verses from Philippians 4:6-7:

"Do not be anxious about anything, but in everything, by prayer and petition, with thanksgiving, present your requests to God. And the peace of God, which transcends all understanding, will guard your hearts and your minds in Christ Jesus."

AUTHOR REFLECTIONS

May you walk boldly with Jesus to wherever He leads you. Even if you only carry a small travel bag.

DISCUSSION QUESTIONS

DISCUSSION ONE

Before Jesus sends out the Twelve, He gives them instructions on what to take on their travels (Mark 6:8-11). Jesus allows only the bare necessities. How would you feel embarking on a trip without money, snacks, or an itinerary?

What purpose did having a staff accomplish?

What is your "staff of comfort" when leaving home?

_____
_____
_____
_____

DISCUSSION TWO

Have you ever traveled somewhere that stretched you as a person, or stretched your faith? Please share it with the group or write the event here. What did you learn from this experience or excursion?

_____

DISCUSSION QUESTIONS

_____
_____
_____

DISCUSSION THREE

Jesus states in Mark 6:4, "Only in his hometown, among his relatives and in his own house is a prophet without honor."

Jesus is fully God and fully Man (Galatians 4:4-5). How do you think He felt when his neighbors and relatives questioned His teaching and authority?

_____
_____
_____
_____

Have you experienced any disrespect or indifference going back to a place where you have lived, worked, or gone to school? Was the disrespect regarding your faith? How did that experience make you feel? How did you grow as a person because of the conflict?

_____
_____
_____
_____

For further study, read Luke 4:14-30. How did the people of Nazareth treat Jesus in this account in the book of Luke?

_____
_____
_____
_____

DISCUSSION QUESTIONS

DISCUSSION FOUR

Did it surprise you that Jesus had brothers and sisters? Why or why not? Which siblings are mentioned in Mark 6:3?

_____
_____
_____
_____

DISCUSSION FIVE

In Mark 6:11, Jesus tells the disciples that if no one welcomes them or listens to them, they should shake the dust off their feet when they leave. What do you think this means?

_____
_____
_____
_____

Read Matthew 12:30. Would the people who rejected the Twelve be for Jesus or against Him?

_____
_____
_____
_____

According to Matthew 10:32-33, what are the people in danger of if they reject Jesus?

_____
_____
_____
_____

DISCUSSION QUESTIONS

DISCUSSION SIX

The stakes are high for those who reject Jesus, yet many in the world do not know about Him. What is the most daring thing you have done to share the love of Jesus with others?

_____
_____
_____
_____

When my brother-in-law suffered with late-stage Alzheimer's disease, he would always say to his caregivers, "I love my Jesus." That simple phrase showed where his hope came from and why, in the midst of suffering, he still had joy. He organically and humbly practiced evangelism by sharing his faith in one sentence.

Evangelism can be uncomfortable, and in some places in the world, life-threatening. Can you think of something you can do this week to shine a light on Jesus or simply add His name into a conversation?

_____
_____
_____
_____

Share your experience with your study group or write it here for future encouragement.

_____
_____
_____
_____

Part FIVE
Finding Fast Food in a Desert

Scripture Passage:
**Mark 6:30-44;
John 6:1-13**

ONE

But he answered, "You give them something to eat."
Mark 6:37a

The disciples relaxed upon stumps placed in a semi-circle around a flat-topped rock occupied by Jesus. Peter scrubbed a hand over his jaw, trying to hide his amusement as Thomas recounted his travels with Judas in the Decapolis. The wind picked up, rustling the olive leaves above the shaded courtyard in Capernaum. Even the bobbing branches seemed giddy at Thomas's story. Thomas gestured wildly as he paced in front of Jesus, eagerly sharing the ministry done around Galilee.

"You should have seen it." Thomas rested a hand upon Judas's shoulder, but Judas shrugged the touch away. "When I grabbed hold and shook a man possessed by demons, a mouse flew out from under the man's sleeve and clung to Judas's tunic. The vermin scurried over his shoulder." Thomas could barely contain his laughter. "I've never seen Judas flail and dance around like a girl."

Peter forced a chuckle to stay buried in his gut. He had seen Matthew spooked by demons in their seaside town, but Matthew hadn't pranced about causing a commotion. He had engaged their attacker with his staff.

"I did not dance." Judas stomped from the shade into the sunlight. "I was trying to rid myself of the animal."

John shifted on his stump of a seat. "Ministry is hard work. It is good to enjoy a lighthearted story."

"At my expense." Judas folded his arms over his tunic and glared at John.

"At all of our expenses." John opened his arms as if to welcome Judas back into the cool shade. "We all have spoken of blessings and curses during our time away. We can relate to this shock." He leaped to his feet and bucked like a bull in front of Jesus and Thomas.

Peter had rarely seen John so carefree, but then, his fellow fisherman liked to keep the peace. John had calmed Peter's ire on more than one occasion, and now he attempted to lighten Judas's mood.

Everyone laughed, including Judas.

Voices and the scuffling of sandals drew Peter's attention to the main thoroughfare through Capernaum. He stepped from the canopy of olive branches. In the distance, he spied at least a dozen men hovering near his home. Two men lingered there a short time ago. More people appeared to be waiting where the road dissolved into the shore. How could the disciples and Jesus return home for a meal without Jesus being urged to heal or teach? Were their boats surrounded by mobs as well? Sooner or later, even with the tree cover, someone would recognize one of them, and a crowd would assemble.

Jesus rose and strode through the middle of their gathering. He pulled down a full branch and beheld the people without a wrinkle on His face or a crease on His forehead. Peter wished he could glean the Savior's thoughts.

Jesus turned toward the circle. "Come with me to a quiet place and get some rest." He strolled from their gathering place, out into the sun, and angled toward the back of the synagogue.

"Where are we going now?" Thomas held out his hands as if he wasn't done telling stories.

Peter hurried to follow Jesus. As he passed Thomas, he said, "You heard Him. To find rest. It won't be quiet in Capernaum. The crowds have found us."

Shaking his head, Judas blew out a loud sigh. "They always find us. Always."

Peter couldn't disagree with his fellow disciple, but the person the crowds were coming to see wasn't as unsettled as Judas.

"You should be happy." Peter clapped a hand on Judas's back. "Since Jesus healed Jairus's daughter, we have use of the synagogue ruler's big boat, and it won't cost us a shekel."

TWO

"Ah." Miriam stutter-stepped, trying not to smash the stone in her right sandal again. She stopped walking on the road toward Bethsaida with one foot halted on tiptoe.

Her husband's eyes widened as he hurried to her side. His satchel bounced against his hip.

"Are you well, wife? Do you need to sit down?" His gaze beheld her as if she might collapse before him. "It isn't …"

"No." She was quick to put his concern to rest. "It isn't." Her poor husband. He didn't know a pebble caused her discomfort and not the baby inside her womb. "There is a stone caught beneath my foot."

He let out a large breath and guided her to a stump at the side of the road. The hill held a few stumps for those who grew weary on the climb. More than the usual number of people ventured over the hilly landscape. Or maybe it was the same number. Her mind had been clouded since …

"Maybe it is a sign you should not be traveling this far." He gently settled her on the flat wooden seat. "I have a cousin who could loan us a donkey."

"Daniel, I will be fine." She forced a smile against the storm of emotions swirling inside her heart. The joy of another baby was shadowed by the loss of their first child. Their precious son had been born too soon. But now she had to assure Daniel she could make it home to Bethsaida, or he would worry every step of the way.

"I have not felt any pains like before. I enjoy accompanying you into town." She removed her sandal and rubbed her skin. The stubborn stone fell to the ground.

Daniel knelt in front of her. "Are you sure?"

"As ever, husband. If your doubts linger, we will stop on the other side of the hill and savor our loaf of bread."

Late afternoon sunlight glistened in his eyes. "If you are certain."

Oh Lord, let me speak this truth for five more months.

"I am sure." She prayed that she was sure enough for it not to be a lie.

Peter dug his oar into the lake as Jesus perched in the front of the boat. Jesus faced southward toward their destination. The hills of Bethsaida would give Jesus a place to hide away. At least for a while.

The wind annoyed the waves, making progress a challenge. Peter's muscles ached from wrestling the water.

"This wind is slowing us down." Judas sat nearest to Peter, an oar in his lap. If the disciple wanted a quick journey, he should lower his oar. "The people are able to follow us on land." Judas scowled as he scanned the edge of the sea.

"And that's a bad thing?" Peter knew his words might goad Judas, but sometimes the man frayed his patience.

Judas's brow furrowed as he turned toward Peter. No doubt an explanation was coming. Judas had an opinion about every matter. So did Peter, but where Jesus was concerned, Peter had learned to defer to their Lord. A flash of heat engulfed Peter's body. He tamped the anger boiling under his skin. Why did Judas have so many complaints?

"How can Jesus hear of our travels if a crowd is seeking Him?" Judas balanced his weight on his oar. "They call out and interrupt Him, and us. Can we not have a moment of peace?"

Peter continued his fight against the waves and against his irritation with his fellow disciple. "If the Lord didn't want them to catch us, He could still the wind." Something Peter's muscles would cheer.

Judas tilted his head toward the waves. "You believe He could do that again?"

"You don't?" How could Judas witness miracle after miracle and not believe that Jesus could do another? The Lord must see something in Judas that Peter did not, for Judas's constant questions festered in Peter's gut.

Sitting straighter, Judas said, "We will never find rest with people clamoring after us." He dipped his paddle into the water, but with the effort he put into his rowing, the boat would likely anchor in place.

Peter cast a glance at the shore, squinting against the afternoon sun. Multitudes followed the course of their boat.

Peter halted his rowing. It did not matter if the disciples battled wind and waves or had a calm sea, the souls on the shore would still seek Jesus. How could Judas be ignorant of that truth?

Another truth struck Peter. Perhaps Jesus wanted the people on the shore to catch the boat. He stifled a grin. For once, he was thinking like Jesus.

Men, women, and children waited at the water's edge as Jesus's boat landed near the main streets of Bethsaida. Even men in fishing boats called out to Jesus as He approached the shore. If disgruntled Judas desired a quiet place, he would have to wander on his own. Peter would not neglect these people who sought Jesus. Not after all the hurt and brokenness he had seen during his travels with Matthew.

The confines of the shore stifled Jesus's teaching. He led the people into the hills near town. Cool winds on the hillside tempered the heat of the day as the sun prepared to linger a few hours more.

Jesus had finished speaking in parables when He sat on a stump, scanning the faces intent for more of His words. Peter waited not far from his Lord as Andrew and John instructed newcomers from the outskirts of Bethsaida where to sit or stand.

Judas and Thomas strode toward Jesus. Other disciples followed.

"This is a remote place, and it's already very late," Judas grumbled. "Send the people away so they can go to the surrounding countryside and buy themselves something to eat."

Peter's stomach gurgled at the mention of food. He had not eaten since morning, and after rowing, his body craved a meal.

"You give them something to eat," Jesus said.

Philip threw up his hands. "Eight months' wages would not buy enough bread for each one to have a bite."

"More than eight months' wages," Judas echoed. "And I do not have that sum in our money bag."

"Are we to spend that much on bread and give it to them to eat?" Matthew had collected tax money. He knew the magnitude of the cost to feed a hungry crowd.

Peter would have to fish for a month to feed this gathering.

Jesus regarded His disciples. "How many loaves do you have? Go and see."

Andrew, Peter's brother, spoke up. "There is a boy with five small barley loaves and two small fish, but how far will they go among so many?"

Silence befell the huddle of disciples. Peter knew the answer to Andrew's question. He prayed they all knew the answer in their hearts.

Jesus didn't need to explain the details. They had seen the Son of God cast out demons and raise the dead. He could feed all of Galilee with or without one small loaf.

Peter broke the silence. "Sounds like plenty of food to me."

THREE

Miriam and Daniel stood near Jesus of Nazareth, hemmed in by an enormous crowd pressing closer to hear Jesus's words. People confessed this man to be the Messiah, and the more He spoke, the more Miriam believed the rumors to be true.

"Husband, did you hear? The followers of Jesus are talking about food." A sudden giddiness, a peace that had fled these past months, engulfed her soul. "We have our loaf to share."

Daniel shook his head. "I am not so sure." He laid a hand over his satchel. "This is the only food we have. What if you become weak from traveling? This loaf is too small to feed these crowds." He met her gaze with a pained expression. "I have to think of you and the baby."

"I know." And she did, for before Jesus had spoken, she would have feared being a good distance from home without a loaf. "I know you are worried, and I was too. But after hearing this man speak, I have comfort. A comfort for the present and for the future. Do you not agree that this man speaks as the Messiah? He does not repeat the words of other rabbis. He speaks with His own authority." She rocked forward hoping her husband experienced the same assuredness from the teachings of Jesus.

A grin played on his lips. "I do, wife. I have never heard such power spoken by a mere man. A crowd of this size cannot be wrong.

My heart says this man is like no other. Who else could He be but our Savior." His hand eased from the rounded satchel. "We should share our bread with His men."

She clasped her hands and smiled at Daniel. Her heart burst with love for the husband God had given her. A righteous man who listened with his head and with his being and always trusted in the teachings of the One True God.

Daniel's hand shot toward the blue sky. "I have bread to share."

A burly disciple strolled to them.

Daniel removed the loaf from his bag. "You may give this to Jesus to feed these people. Our neighbors." Daniel cleared his throat as he handed the loaf to the broad man. "If there is extra, my wife is with child."

The disciple grinned. "From what I have seen with my eyes, I know our Lord can do much with what I believe is a little. I am thankful for your offering, but Jesus has received five barley loaves and two fish. He is able to bless the food abundantly. The Lord will provide what you need. I know this to be true. *Toda raba*."

"We will await His blessing." Daniel nodded and returned the loaf to his satchel.

She smiled at her husband.

"I feel an anticipation that I have never experienced. Not before our last child, or this one." Her chin dropped to indicate her belly.

"My love, I know of what you speak. We will watch and wait, for there are people as far as the eye can see. Jesus has invited us to listen, and He is going to host a feast for His guests."

And that was the conundrum that kept her standing on a hillside in the sun. For she did not worry about the crowds, or the lack of food, on this remote hill. Her spirit was calm and filled with elation at being in the presence of a man who taught with power and authority, and with an assured belief that His listeners would be satisfied with the food His followers offered.

FOUR

Jesus surveyed the hillside and beamed at the people waiting to hear His next word.

A shiver of elation streaked through Peter's body. His skin chilled the same as when the Lord calmed the storm on the sea. Jesus prepared to make five loaves and two fish feed thousands. Would it be any harder to multiply bread than to banish the wind or heal the sick? Of course not. He barked out a laugh.

"Peter!" Judas's voice returned Peter's mind to the grassy hill. "Were you listening?"

With my heart.

"We need to have the people sit down in groups of fifty and a hundred."

Peter pressed his lips together to contain an outburst. Hadn't Moses numbered the people in the wilderness in a similar way? His heart clamored while waiting for Jesus to perform another miracle. Judas was too preoccupied to understand that Jesus didn't care about coins, or how much a feast for thousands would cost. Jesus cared about each and every soul sitting in the grass.

"I will do as the Lord wishes, Judas. We will plant gardens of people on this hill and feed them."

Judas passed by and muttered, "I would have sent them away."

Smiling like a bridegroom, Peter shouted instructions to the crowd. The Son of the Most High God was orchestrating a banquet. The Lord was going to unleash His goodness on these people.

When the crowd was divided according to the Lord's command, Jesus gathered the five loaves in one arm and held the two fish in His other hand. He looked to heaven and gave thanks. Setting the bread and fish on a stump, He broke the bread and handed part of the loaves to Peter and the other disciples. The Lord also removed pieces of fish and made sure each disciple had a portion.

Peter stared at the piece of fish almost three fingers wide. How could this feed his grouping of fifty? No. He would not doubt. The amount would be enough. Jesus always made sure they had enough.

Dropping to his knees before a cluster of families, Peter rested the fish on his thigh and began tearing pieces of bread to offer to the men, women, and children. He bestowed a portion on a bearded man, his wife, and his two children, and extended pieces for another family. More bread appeared for Daniel and his wife. Over and over, each hand accepted nourishment. Peter laughed heartily as everyone received enough bread to eat.

He lifted the fish off of his thigh, anticipating the joy of seeing something he regarded as an ordinary commodity, a smelly fish, become a banquet meal for the crowd. A delicacy of flaky fillets satisfied every person. The enormity of the amount of food that surrounded him left him speechless. If his hands did not stink of fish, and crumbs did not cling to his tunic, he would have been skeptical that such an abundance was possible from so little. His cheeks ached from the honor of taking part in Jesus's compassion. Thousands of people were satisfied with scarcely enough bread and fish to feed three families.

After the food had been distributed, Peter lounged in the grass and ate. Bread and fish. Fish and bread. His stomach savored the freshest food he had ever tasted.

Later, he carried a basketful of leftovers to Jesus. Each of the disciples carried a similar basket overflowing with bread and fish. Twelve baskets of leftovers from almost no food at all. An abundance. A miracle. Another day with Jesus.

A full loaf of bread balanced at the edge of Matthew's basket.

Peter dropped his basket and took his friend's loaf. "I have need of this."

Even though his arms burned, and his feet complained about each new step, he sprinted east. His heart pounded so hard it nearly clogged his chest. He raced onward, scanning the crowds because when God brought someone to mind, it was best not to dismiss the blessing.

FIVE

Daniel helped his wife to her feet. Her eyes blinked from the brightness of the setting sun as she met his gaze.

"Can you believe it, husband? We received more fish and bread than we could eat. I believed Jesus would care for us, but I did not expect so much for so many."

He held on to her hand, relishing its softness and warmth.

"God provided manna for our forefathers in the desert, and Jesus has provided for us on this hillside. If I am asked about this man, I must declare that He is the Messiah." He gestured, indicating the dispersing crowd. "How could a mere man feed this many people if not by a miracle of God?"

"I believe you, husband. I believe in Jesus." Miriam squeezed his hand and flashed a mesmerizing smile.

"Daniel," a man shouted.

Peter, a follower of Jesus, and the man who had given food to their group sprinted toward him. He stopped and bent to catch his breath. In his hand was a complete loaf of bread.

"Daniel, your wife is expecting a child. May I offer you additional bread for your journey?"

Pressure tingled behind Daniel's eyes. The events of the day had exhausted his emotions, in a good manner, but he was only flesh and bone. "*Toda raba*, Peter. Our bellies are full, but we will save this gift and thank God when we break it anew. We will remember this day and the teachings of Jesus."

"That is all I ask." Peter bowed. "My fellow disciples await my return. May the Lord bless you and your wife." Peter acknowledged Miriam. "Oh, and may the Lord bless your son."

Daniel pressed a hand to his chest. A reply faltered on his lips.

"Farewell, Daniel and family." Peter turned and ran toward Jesus.

Miriam gripped his sleeve. "Did you hear that, husband? Peter said we are going to have a son." She rocked backward as if she were going to faint.

Daniel supported her and gathered his strength. For if he contemplated the events of this day, he might faint too.

AUTHOR REFLECTIONS

The miracle of the feeding of the five thousand appears in all four Gospels—Matthew, Mark, Luke, and John. Mark and Matthew give us a fast-paced narrative, but Luke and John add some details to the account. We know that more than five thousand people would have been fed due to Matthew 14:21.

The number of those who ate was about five thousand men, besides women and children.

John also mentions the crowd size in John 6:10.

Luke tells us that the feeding of the crowd happens in Bethsaida (Luke 9:10). This town sits on the shores of the Sea of Galilee not far from Capernaum. John lets us know in John 1:44 that Peter, Andrew, and Philip were from Bethsaida. Is that why Andrew is aware of the boy with the bread and fish? John also writes that it is Philip who blurts out about the food costing eight months' wages. The other disciples agree with Philip's assessment, so everyone is aghast at the cost of feeding so many.

Throughout Jesus's ministry, His home base is in Capernaum where Peter's house is located. We do not know when Peter and Andrew made the move from Bethsaida to Capernaum.

Was I too hard on Judas in this story? While Philip blurts out about the cost of feeding the crowd, Judas may have gripped the money bag

AUTHOR REFLECTIONS

tight. We are told by John that Judas liked to help himself to the disciples' funds as Judas was the "keeper of the money bag" (John 12:1-8). Since Judas ultimately betrays Jesus for thirty pieces of silver, I had fun making him disgruntled when Jesus suggests feeding the masses on the disciples' dime.

Jesus says to His disciples, "You give them something to eat." There is no mention of a collection from the people. I'm sure some of the crowd traveled with snacks, but Jesus doesn't ask them to part with their food. He is providing abundantly for the needs of the crowd.

Not only is Jesus providing a meal, but He is also speaking with power and authority. Jesus doesn't need to quote a rabbi or prophet. He is the Son of the Most High God. Jesus is The Word of God. John tells us this in John 1:1-2.

In the beginning was the Word, and the Word was with God, and the Word was God. He was with God in the beginning.

When I traveled around the Sea of Galilee, we stopped in the hilly countryside and were taught in a natural amphitheater. Our teacher stood at the bottom of the hill, and we sat on the slope. We were able to hear every word. If we had done the reverse, our teacher at the top of the hill and students at the bottom, the wind would have carried our instruction away. We aren't told exactly what part of the hill Jesus taught from in Mark's account, or the other Gospels.

I do find it interesting that the people were able to chase after Jesus's boat and catch up with Him. It may have been a windy day, and the wind slowed Jesus's progression. He could have taken care of the wind, but He allowed the trip to be delayed and for the people to catch the boat. If it was windy, Jesus wouldn't have wanted to teach from the top of the hill.

Ultimately, this miracle shows Jesus's power, but also His compassion. Jesus cared about the empty bellies that sat around Him, and He knew they needed more than just bread. They needed the Bread of Life, Jesus, their Savior. He gave of Himself fully to a weary crowd of travelers.

Shortly after this miracle in the Gospel of John, Jesus declares to His disciples, "I am the bread of life" (John 6:35).

I hope you remember this story the next time you see a loaf of bread. Jesus held a banquet with five loaves and two fish. The Bread of Life gave abundantly to all who listened to His words. May we always be ready to listen to Jesus. He gives us life abundantly, and eternally.

DISCUSSION QUESTIONS

DISCUSSION ONE

Are you a people person? Does conversing with several people at a gathering drain your energy or energize your spirit?

_____
_____
_____
_____

During the disciples' debriefing with Jesus, we are told so many people were coming and going that Jesus and His disciples didn't have time to eat (Mark 6:30-31).

Because of the vast number of people, Jesus takes the disciples to a quiet place to rest. What does this say about His humanity?

Why is it crucial to rest when you deal with the needs of other people?

_____
_____
_____

DISCUSSION QUESTIONS

Have you experienced a time in your life when rest was elusive? How did you feel? Did certain areas of your life suffer during this time?

DISCUSSION TWO

Jesus has compassion on the lost sheep seeking His teaching. The Bible tells us that Jesus is our Good Shepherd. Read John 10:1-18 and Matthew 26:31-32.

What tasks does a shepherd perform? Do you see some of those tasks performed in this story by Jesus and the disciples? What did Jesus ultimately do for His sheep?

DISCUSSION THREE

What are the disciples worried about according to Mark 6:35-36? Are the disciples justified in their worry? Do the disciples underestimate Jesus's power?

DISCUSSION QUESTIONS

Have you ever experienced something in your life that you didn't know how it was going to work out, but Jesus orchestrated an amazing outcome? Note it here and share about it if you desire.

_____
_____
_____
_____

DISCUSSION FOUR

What does Jesus do before He breaks the loaves and prepares the food?

Do you regularly give thanks before a meal? Are you consistent about saying grace even in public? Share a favorite grace or prayer.

_____
_____
_____
_____

Prayers of gratitude do not have to be fancy. They can be a simple heartfelt thank you.

My simple grace:

Thank you, Lord, for this food and for the people around this table. May You bless this food to our bodies, so we may do Your work.

Amen

_____
_____
_____
_____

DISCUSSION FIVE

We are not given the reactions of the disciples as they assessed their

DISCUSSION QUESTIONS

provisions and then dispersed to feed the masses. Do you believe they expected a miracle? Why or why not?

_____
_____
_____
_____

What was left over after the five thousand men (and the additional women and children) ate their fill? How does this speak to God's abundance in our lives? What is the ultimate abundant gift? Consider Matthew 6:26 and II Peter 1:1-2.

_____
_____
_____
_____

DISCUSSION SIX

Fellowship and community can be cultivated over a meal. We can encourage fellow believers and also build relationships with unbelievers while we eat together. The Bible tells us to practice hospitality. See Romans 12:13 and I Peter 4:9-11.

Is practicing hospitality easy for you? What holds you back from inviting people into your home?

_____
_____
_____
_____

Consider reaching out to someone this week by baking them bread or cookies. You can always invite them over for a meal or take them out to dinner. Don't forget to say, "Do you mind if I bless the food?"

Part SIX
Casting from Afar

Scripture Passage:
Mark 7:24-30

ONE

Jesus left that place and went to the vicinity of Tyre. He entered a house and did not want anyone to know it; yet he could not keep his presence secret.
Mark 7:24

Engulfed in shadows, Peter lingered in the alley beside the stone carver's door. He squinted into the darkness and scanned the road to town. No one had followed him from the baker's home. He pretended to arrange loaves in his satchel. Dawn's shadows remained calm. Giddiness enlivened his mood. For once, they were alone. In his mind, he had questioned traveling north to Tyre, but Jesus was right. He was always right. The religious leaders squawked among themselves in the southern city of Jerusalem. In Tyre, no chief priest or elder came to the door to question Jesus. The spies sent by the teachers of the law did not crouch in the bushes, waiting to hurl accusations.

Peter opened the door. John reclined in the corner, his lips moving as if in prayer. On the other side of the room, disciples slept soundly. Their snores immitated a soothing harp song. His fellow disciples rarely slept undisturbed by those seeking Jesus.

John opened his eyes and gestured toward the street. His fingers danced to indicate if a crowd had followed.

Grinning, Peter shook his head. He could almost hear distant shouts of Jesus's name or the thudding footsteps of friends carrying the sick on mats, but not this morning. The day ahead could be filled with fellowship, food, and more teaching from the Lord. His list of questions grew by the day. One thing was settled. He knew for sure that Jesus was the Christ. The Messiah walked the hills of Galilee beside him. With that certainty in his being, he turned his concerns to whether the stone carver's wife had enough oil and herbs for dipping their bread.

TWO

Amina wiped her brow. The day started warmer than usual. She and her husband set out their wares in the marketplace. Small jars of olive oil and decorated lamps lined their table. At the far end of the booth, hunched over her ink well, their daughter Yara created designs to adorn stone lamps and wooden beads. The growing bustle of travelers to Tyre and the loud bartering of customers didn't disturb her daughter. Yara inked perfect shapes without patterns cut from parchment.

A woman strolled by their booth. Her wheat-colored braids were tucked under an embroidered head covering. The muted mustard-colored threads contrasted with the dark charcoal lining her brown eyes. The woman halted in front of Yara and smiled.

Engrossed in her work, Yara didn't acknowledge the woman's presence. Amina would talk to her later about pleasantries. At Yara's young age, she had more to learn about engaging with customers and completing a sale.

"Are you interested in a lamp?" Amina held out one of Yara's most intricate designs. "My daughter is talented. She inks the designs on all of our wares."

The woman drew her hand over the tops of the lamps. Gold rings glistened in the early morning light.

"I can see your daughter is a fine artisan."

Amina squared her shoulders at the woman's praise. "Yara, what do you say to these kind words?"

Yara glanced up from her brushwork and blinked at the woman. "I am happy that you like them." She rose and shifted toward the beaded necklaces. "I painted these as well." She beamed at their customer.

So her daughter had learned a few ways of selling more goods.

"I most definitely will take one of your necklaces." The woman fingered the wooden beads. "You are pretty like your mother. Dark hair and eyes the color of a raven's wing." She laughed. "You both likely hear that often."

Yara squinted at the woman. "Thank you." Her voice squeaked as if she didn't believe the flattery. She returned to her patterns.

"You are too kind." Amina bobbed her head. How could this woman think her beautiful when her face glowed from the heat.

The woman slipped a necklace over her head covering and arranged the beads to accentuate their designs. She also chose a lamp and handed Amina a gold coin that covered the cost of more than three necklaces and three lamps.

Amina's heartbeat quickened. Did her husband have coins to repay the difference so early in the day?

"You have given us too much. I will get my husband to make your change."

She stepped to where her husband spoke with the man from the next booth.

"Husband," she whispered, trying to be discreet. "I have need of a few coins. This woman has given me too much in gold." She opened her hand to show the thick coin.

Her husband frowned as he cast a glance at the table. Was his pouch empty? Her stomach hollowed.

"What woman? I do not see a customer."

Amina spun toward the table, but the woman was gone. Yara remained steadfast in her work.

"Daughter, where did our customer go?"

Yara looked up. Her eyes grew wide. "I thought she went with you to see father."

Her daughter leaned over the table, scanned the row of booths, and shrugged.

Amina bit her lip. How strange. In all her years as a merchant, she had never had a customer pay more than what was owed. Her skin pimpled. It wasn't right to keep the gold. She hurried into the street and observed the line of booths, attempting to spot the woman. Their elegant customer was nowhere in sight. She couldn't have vanished. Amina's skin shivered. What an unusual way to start their morning.

THREE

"Yara, come with me to the well." Noor hurried toward their booth. An empty water jar hung from her hand.

Yara set down her brush. She stood and stretched her muscles. A short trip to the well would do her legs good. She enjoyed passing time with her friend.

"Mother, can I go with Noor and fill our jug?"

Her mother cut a wick and handed it to a customer. "Hurry back. We are busy today with the crowds."

Yara grabbed a water jar and joined Noor. They jogged the main road through Tyre, dodging the mass of people bartering for goods.

Noor veered to the right.

"Come this way. It is shorter." Noor slowed to a walk in the alleyway behind the temple.

Yara followed, but her mind echoed her mother's warnings about what women and girls did inside the temple in service to the gods.

"My mother doesn't like me to go this way." She hastened her steps. The sooner they passed the temple, the better.

"Don't worry. We are not stopping." Noor continued down the alley with her jar nestled on her hip.

As they neared an overhang, a woman stepped from the shade. Her outstretched arm held a burning lamp.

"Yara?"

The customer from earlier was holding the lamp she had purchased. She sauntered closer. "Look at the fire, young one." She held the lamp in front of Yara's face.

The scent of the burning oil tickled Yara's nose. Why had the woman remembered her name? Yara's skin chilled as she glanced at the beautiful stranger. She didn't want to be rude, so she stared at the flame.

"Do you know her?" Noor waited a few steps away.

The woman scowled at Noor. "It is her design. Look at your pattern, Yara. It's dancing under the flame. Do you see it?"

Yara blinked as the colors of the flame brightened.

"Look harder, Yara." The woman's features grew larger in front of Yara's face. "Do you feel the heat from the flame? Empty your mind and allow the fire to delight you."

"We need to go." Noor tugged on the back of Yara's tunic.

"She bought my lamp." Yara didn't want to insult the woman. Father still owed her money. She concentrated on the flickering flame.

"Yes. Open your mind, girl. Let the inferno inside."

A strange hissing erupted from the lamp.

Startled, Yara tried to step away, but her legs stiffened. She couldn't escape from the fire. As she breathed in the warmth of the reddish flame, something smothered her breath. She needed air, but her lungs burned from an oppressive heat.

"Keep your mind open, Yara," the woman shouted. "Open and free."

Yara's eyesight danced with sparks from the flickering lamplight as she choked out a wheeze. She needed air. A shadow darkened her vision.

Noor screamed.

Yara wanted to scream, too, but she was falling. An eerie cackling echoed in her ears. She struck the dirt, and her jar tumbled from her grasp. Why had the sun turned black?

FOUR

Amina tore through the crowd in the wake of her husband. He barked commands at the buyers dawdling in their path.

Her throat burned, restricting her breathing, but she would not stop running. She had to find Yara.

Noor's hysteria had relayed all that mattered. Yara had been attacked by a spirit. An evil spirit. How could this happen to Yara in the light of day?

That woman. How could that woman have betrayed Yara? She was a child. Amina stifled a sob. She had to reach her daughter.

Nearing the temple's rear alleyway, her husband pointed and shouted at the woman dragging Yara from the alley.

Her daughter did not thrash or move. She lay as lifeless as a corpse.

A fiery hatred engulfed Amina's body. She charged the woman like a mad bull.

The woman released Yara and fled toward the temple. Amina did not follow. Yara was her only daughter and needed help.

"What happened to my daughter?" Amina shouted as she knelt beside Yara. She did not get an answer from the fleeing coward.

"Yara. Yara, speak to me." She patted her daughter's face, but Yara did not answer. Her eyes stared into the distance. The heat of a fever colored her cheeks crimson.

Her husband lifted Yara off the ground and slung her over his shoulder. She hung limp down his back.

This tragedy could not be happening. The day had started out so well with abundant sales. Her daughter went on a harmless trip with a friend to fill a water jar. She staggered after her husband. They needed to go home. And then what? Sorrow constricted her breaths.

"Amina." The baker's wife came alongside her. "I know someone who may be able to assist you."

A hiccup stuttered from Amina's mouth. "Who can help us now? An evil spirt is inside of my daughter." Panic rose within her breast while tears streamed down her cheeks.

"Listen to me." The baker's wife grabbed hold of Amina's shoulder. "I know who can save Yara."

Slowing her rush home, Amina stared at this woman who uttered such a bold assurance. Could what this woman said be true? Amina's whole body trembled. "Who but the God of all gods can help my daughter now?"

Her fellow merchant's eyes filled with tears. "I know where the God of all gods is staying."

FIVE

Peter attempted to repair a rip in his cloak. If only his wife were here in Tyre. Her nimble fingers would have restored the weave before it had unraveled this far.

The peaceful afternoon had several of his fellow disciples resting. A few took discreet walks through town. He concentrated on securing a stitch while Jesus reclined nearby.

He stilled his needle. Had he heard a shout? Or was his mind replaying the many summons hurled at Jesus? Week after week, day after day, people called out to capture Jesus's attention.

"Lord, have mercy," a shrill voice cried.

Peter rolled his head backward and flung his cloak aside. He hadn't imagined the sounds. Couldn't Jesus be left alone for one day? He glanced at Jesus. The Lord's eyes fluttered open.

A rapid pounding assaulted the wooden door.

Peter leaped to his feet. Andrew entered from a side room and followed him to the door.

The rapping grew louder.

"Lord, Son of David, have mercy on me!"

More banging. Peter cast a glance at Andrew, who shrugged.

"Lord, I beg of you, help me. My daughter is suffering." The woman's emboldened pleas would disturb anyone in the vicinity of their house.

Jesus strolled toward the door.

"If I don't let her in," Peter said, "she is likely to break through the wood."

Jesus swept an arm toward the threshold as if ushering in a nobleman.

Peter broadened his stance and opened the door.

A wide-eyed, red-cheeked woman blocked the entrance to their home, her hand raised for another knock.

"Lord," she gasped, rushing into the room. "I beg of You. Heal my daughter."

Philip and Thomas rushed into the corridor outside the house and waited. Did they wonder if restraint would be needed?

The distraught mother fell at Jesus's feet. "Help me," she wailed.

Peter rubbed a hand over his face and pinched his chin. He'd seen women overcome with grief, but this woman's torment rivaled any other. And where was her daughter? Would they need to travel a distance to heal her? His mind cluttered with emotions and practical tasks.

Jesus beheld the woman slumped at his feet.

"Send her away, for she keeps crying out after us," Jesus said.

Andrew laid a hand on Peter's shoulder. Had his brother sensed his inner conflict? Was he volunteering to remove the stranger? Or simply offering consolation? How much more despair would they witness?

"Drive out the demon, Lord." The woman rocked back on her heels and beseeched Jesus. Her regard held the determination of a conniving tax collector.

Jesus did not extend a hand of comfort. Why was the Lord stoic? The mother continued to weep, but the Lord offered no soothing words as He had before with Jairus's wife or the woman in Capernaum who touched his hem.

"First let the children eat all they want," Jesus told her. "For it is not right to take the children's bread and toss it to their dogs."

Peter coughed. Had the Lord called this woman a dog?

Andrew shifted closer to their visitor. The insult was not lost on Philip or Thomas, whose shocked expressions must mirror his own.

When had Jesus ever denied a humble beggar who sought healing?

Peter's forehead succumbed to a thunderous ache. He must have more to learn.

———

Amina shook her head. She would not agree with Jesus's assessment. In her heart, she knew this man was God. She had heard of His miracles for months, but the testimony of her neighbor confirmed her belief. Jesus of Nazareth was the Son of God.

Her belly churned like a choppy sea. She knew her only hope towered above her. She didn't need a loaf of bread from the Lord, she only needed a scrap of His power.

Gazing upward from her kneel, she studied every wrinkle on the Lord's face.

"Yes, Lord." She hiccupped. "But even the dogs under the table eat the children's crumbs." *Believe me, Lord. For I believe in You.*

The Lord's mouth curved ever so slightly. Was that a glimmer of understanding in His eyes? She squeezed her hands together and pressed them to her lips. She would remain and plead her case for Yara. *Yara!* Tears threatened to douse her cheeks anew.

"For such a reply, you may go. The demon has left your daughter."

Tears moistened the fingers covering her mouth.

"Thank you, Lord." She attempted to smile, but her lips quivered. "Your crumbs are enough for me."

She crawled toward the door, careful not to touch the men hovering around her. When the sun warmed her back, she rose and sprinted toward her home.

"Yara, I'm coming," she yelled to the wind. "I'm coming to you." The gusts blew tears of elation from her cheeks. The Lord had healed her daughter, and He wasn't even near their dwelling. Her heart warmed as if the sun blazed within.

Ignoring the ache in her feet, she continued to run, pounding the dirt beneath her sandals.

"Yara," she called, bursting through the doorway to her house. She slid to a halt before her daughter's bedside.

Her husband leaned forward on a stool on the other side of the bed while Yara reclined against a pillow, dipping bread in oil.

"The demon is gone." Her husband's voice caught as he spoke. "I heard a rushing wind, and then Yara jerked forward and told me the Lord had healed her. I have never seen her so … so … alive."

Amina crumpled to the floor and wrapped her daughter in a consuming embrace. "I met the Lord, Jesus, and He healed you." Amina's voice swelled with emotion as she spoke of the miracle that Jesus had commanded.

"How did he do that, Mother?" Yara kissed her cheek and snuggled against her neck.

Joy filled Amina's body. A joy vast and overflowing. She had never been this jubilant and confident before meeting Jesus.

"I don't know, Daughter." She kissed the tip of Yara's nose. "But He did it without a word or a touch. All the way from town."

"I know how He did it." Yara shifted in Amina's arms and smiled her carefree smile. "He did it with His love."

AUTHOR REFLECTIONS

When I first read this account of the desperate mother in the Gospels of Mark and Matthew, I thought, *Ouch*, before I thought, *Praise the Lord*. Jesus's words to this Gentile mother seem harsh. But He is remaining true to His mission. Jesus came to restore His relationship with the children of Israel. This woman doesn't protest the words of Jesus. She doesn't get mad. She shows she is a child of the kingdom even though she isn't of Jewish descent.

The Gentile woman, Amina in my story, remains true to her mission as a persistent and heartbroken mother. She is not going to stop pleading for the healing of her demon-possessed daughter. She knows that Jesus has the power and compassion to restore her. We don't know how she heard about Jesus or how big her initial faith is in Jesus, but we see her faith in action. She is willing to take Jesus's crumbs of compassion, believing they are enough to heal her daughter.

In the Gospel of Mark, the only person to address Jesus as Lord is this desperate mother. The other Gospels use this title for Jesus, but Mark recounts it in the words of a Gentile mom. Somehow she understands the mission of Jesus and desires to be part of it. The overflow of Jesus's mercy is poured out on this woman and her daughter.

In this story, we have the account of the remarkable power of Jesus.

AUTHOR REFLECTIONS

Without being in the same room as the young girl, possibly without being in the same city, and without this girl being from a lost tribe of Israel, Jesus exorcises a demon from her. He announces that the demon has left. We don't see Jesus cast out the demon. We don't see what the healing looked like to those who were in the same room as the little girl. We don't even see how the exorcism went down. We do see that Jesus heals both Jew and Gentile alike. Jesus healed a multitude of people during His ministry around the Sea of Galilee.

Jesus is fully God and fully Man. We see both of these aspects in this biblical account. The human side of Jesus needs rest, but the Son of God reigns over the power of Satan with a thought.

I started this project with the story about a demon-possessed man in Gergasa who was a Gentile. My intent was not to begin and end this study with stories about demons. Perhaps God had another plan. First, we see a demon tell us who Jesus is in Mark 5. Jesus is the Son of the Most High God. In this account, we see that same Son of the Most High God heal and cast out a demon without even speaking a word. I like to call these healings "remote-control" healings because Jesus is so all-powerful over His Creation that He can speak a healing, or think a healing.

In Matthew 15:28, Jesus commends the mother's faith. How did she have such amazing faith that she sought Jesus and lightly debated his initial refusal? We aren't told in the Bible.

We also aren't told how this young girl became possessed by a demon. You might wonder how I crafted my story. I drew on an experience I had before I became a follower of Jesus. Like the little girl in this story, I had a mother with a strong faith in Jesus.

In my pre-teen years, I took martial arts lessons. I wasn't very good, but it was something to pass the time and hang out with my friends. We practiced in a detached dojo near the teacher's house. Everything was going along fine, or so it seemed.

After a lesson, the teacher instructed us to sit in a circle around a lit candle. The room darkened, and we were told to stare at the flame and open our minds. If I was a Christian at this time, I would have been a baby Christian and certainly not skilled in detecting spiritual warfare.

My mother came to pick me up. She was a new believer in Jesus.

AUTHOR REFLECTIONS

The door to the dojo was locked, and the room was dark. My mother could see a candle glowing through the window. Immediately, a chill descended upon her body, and she started praying to God.

A man appeared alongside my mom and began pounding on the dojo door. His parking space was blocked by a car, and he wanted the car moved. Whose car was keeping him from leaving? You guessed it, my mom's.

The dojo door opened, and words ensued. The candle-staring, open-your-mind session ended.

I continued with my martial arts training, but my mom made sure I did not participate in the mind-expanding candle-focus exercise. Several other children were pulled from the séance atmosphere as well.

Harmless or harmful? We need to be on our guard and watch out for the devil's schemes.

We are warned of this in I Peter 5:8-9.

"Be self-controlled and alert. Your enemy the devil prowls around like a roaring lion looking for someone to devour. Resist him, standing firm in the faith, because you know that your brothers throughout the world are undergoing the same kind of sufferings."

I drew on my dojo experience for Amina and Yara's story. I would like to say that the occurrence in the dojo was my only experience with spiritual warfare or demons, but it wasn't. My friends, be on your guard and listen to the convictions of the Holy Spirit. I am thankful my mother loved Jesus, was discerning, and listened to the Spirit's warning.

We continue to struggle against evil in this world. Events and happenings that may seem innocuous can turn dark if one isn't careful. We see this battle between Jesus and Satan throughout the Gospels, but the battle isn't over, even though we know who wins. Jesus is victorious over Satan.

Traveling around the Sea of Galilee where Jesus walked was a highlight of my life. I have never felt so much peace as when I stood where Jesus performed some of His miracles. I hope you have enjoyed this study. I hope you know deep in your heart that we serve a God

AUTHOR REFLECTIONS

more wonderful than I could describe with a few overused adjectives. I hope the wonder and power and love of Jesus shines through in these lessons.

I have lived a life without the presence of Jesus, and I have lived a life with His presence. Living with Jesus as my Lord and Savior is infinitely more unfathomable and, plainly, so much better. I pray you will feel the love of Jesus too. There's more on that blessing after the discussion questions.

To God be the glory.

DISCUSSION QUESTIONS

DISCUSSION ONE

In Mark 7:1-8, Jesus spars with the Pharisees and teachers of the law who had traveled from Jerusalem to question Him. Why might He want to leave Capernaum, a heavily Jewish city, and travel thirty miles north to the Gentile city of Tyre?

Why doesn't Jesus find peace and anonymity in Tyre?

_____
_____
_____
_____

DISCUSSION TWO

Read this account of a desperate mother in Matthew 15:21-28. What does Matthew add in his account that speaks to the faith of the woman?

DISCUSSION QUESTIONS

_____
_____
_____
_____

Does Jesus's initial response to the Syrophoenician woman seem harsh? Would you respond to Jesus if He initially refused your request? Why or why not? How do you respond when your prayers are not answered in a way you would like?

_____
_____
_____
_____

Rahab and Ruth are both women of faith who, like this Syrophoenician woman, were not from the tribes of Israel. Rahab and Ruth are in the line of King David and ultimately the line of Mary and Joseph, then Jesus. Are you familiar with these two ladies?

You can find Rahab's faith in Joshua 2:1-21, and Ruth's faith in the book of Ruth.

Mary and Joseph's lineage is in Matthew 1:16 and Luke 1:26-33.

_____
_____
_____
_____

DISCUSSION THREE

In this healing, we see Jesus cast out a demon and restore a child's health without being in the same room or touching the person. He doesn't even speak the expulsion. Where else in Scripture do we see these types of "remote-control" healings?

Need a hint? Read Matthew 8:5-13 and John 4:46-54.

DISCUSSION QUESTIONS

_____
_____
_____
_____

What do you learn about Jesus from these accounts? In our first lesson, a legion of demons refers to Jesus by His name and title. Do you remember what they called Jesus? Who do you say Jesus is?

_____
_____
_____
_____

DISCUSSION FOUR

What names has Jesus been called in these stories in Mark? Is there a name of Jesus that is special to you?

_____
_____
_____
_____

Look up Jesus's "I AM" statements in the book of John. Write the name given in each verse below.

- John 6:35
- John 8:12
- John 10:7
- John 10:11
- John 11:25
- John 14:6
- John 15:1

DISCUSSION QUESTIONS

_____
_____
_____
_____

DISCUSSION FIVE

Was there a story in this collection that was new to you? Did you learn something new about a familiar story? Share your insights with your study group or write them here.

_____
_____
_____
_____

DISCUSSION SIX

Psalm 62:1-2 tells us where our salvation comes from.

My soul finds rest in God alone;
My salvation comes from him.
He alone is my rock and my salvation;
He is my fortress, I will never be shaken. (NIV)

Are you trusting in Jesus for your salvation? Share a short testimony on how you became a believer in Jesus.

_____
_____
_____
_____

If you're not sure if you are a Christian, a follower of Jesus, Son of the Most High God, then you can find out why Jesus gave His life for you and how you can become a Christ follower in five verses. These verses from lesson one bear repeating.

THE ROMANS ROAD

Romans 3:23, 6:23, 5:8, 10:9-10

_____

_____

_____

_____

What is the Good News or Gospel about Jesus?

Sin separates us from a holy God. Sin doesn't have to be egregious. We sin every day with angry thoughts, hurtful words, or even with actions we don't comprehend as sinful.

The good news is that Jesus paid the price for our sin by shedding His blood on the cross, dying, and rising to life. The blood of the Son of the Most High God paid the price for all the times we blow it. Jesus paid it all, as the hymn says.

When we trust Jesus as our Lord and Savior, we receive a traveling companion, the Holy Spirit. The work of the Spirit is vast and wide, and I would have to write another book to explain all that the Spirit does for us.

We can have a relationship with Jesus that is real every day. Jesus is as alive as He was when he strolled the hills around Capernaum. All you need is faith in Him. You don't need a religious pedigree, a perfect life, or commendable works. Jesus's faithful companions were from all walks of life with their flaws and faults on full display in God's Word.

Jump in the boat with Jesus. Life won't always be smooth sailing, but we know who can calm the storms and get us across the lake.

Thank you for taking this journey with me around the Sea of Galilee.

May the Lord bless you and keep you.

Barbara

FOLLOWING JESUS

Based on Romans 10:9, declare with your mouth that Jesus is Lord and believe in your heart that God raised Him from the dead.

Next steps on your faith journey:

- Study the Bible, especially the New Testament, as it shares the story of Jesus and His church.
- Find a church that preaches from the Word of God and about Jesus.
- If you haven't been baptized, now's the time to pursue baptism (Romans 6:4).
- Enjoy this story from Acts 16:25-34 about a jailer who discovered Jesus and was baptized.

ACKNOWLEDGMENTS

I am humbled and blessed to be writing about my Lord and Savior, Jesus. Without His sinless life and sacrifice, this book would not have been possible.

My family has been my best cheering section throughout my publishing career. I am blessed to have their love, encouragement, and total support.

A big thank you goes to Linda Fulkerson and Liana George for publishing my first foray into combining fiction with nonfiction. The Scrivenings Press family gave me a warm welcome. I am thankful for my editor, Suzie Waltner, who makes me a better writer.

My critique partners, Kathy Zdanowski and Denise Cychosz, cheered me on during the writing of my study. Their encouragement over the years, along with Sandy Goldsworthy, has kept me writing through challenging times.

The author communities of ACFW, ACFW-Wisconsin, FHLCW, SCBWI, Pelican Book Group, and Scrivenings Press have been a huge support in my writing career. The original Brainstormers kept me writing through several rejections. Thank you, Betsy Norman, Karen Miller, Sandee Turriff, and Jill Bevers.

I was blessed to sit under inspiring teaching while in Israel. My husband and I traveled with his alma mater, Dallas Theological Seminary. We sat under the teaching of President Dr. Mark Yarbrough and Systematic Theology professor, Dr. Michael Svigel. I am grateful to our friends Mark and Rhonda Wright, who encouraged us to journey with them to Israel.

My church family has kept me going during good times and troubling times. What a blessing to have their loving support.

Praise to the Lord God Almighty for giving me the gift of creativity and breath each day to write these stories. I am a cancer survivor, and not a day goes by that I don't praise the Lord for His healing. To God be the glory.

ABOUT THE AUTHOR

Barbara M. Britton not only loves to write about the Bible, but she has taught Bible stories for over thirty years. She is multi-published in Christian Fiction, where she brings little-known Bible stories to light or makes readers swoon with her sweet romances. She has a nutrition degree from Baylor University but loves to dip healthy strawberries in chocolate.

Barbara lives in Wisconsin with her husband of almost four decades and an indulged cat. Her sons are grown, but they still come home and request their favorite recipes. Barbara has been a finalist in the prestigious Carol Awards, Reader's Choice Awards, Angel Book Awards, and the National Excellence in Story Telling Contest. You can find out more about Barbara and her books on her website barbarambritton.com.

YOU MAY ALSO LIKE ...

New Star: **Book One of** *The Magi's Encounters*

How far would you go to protect what you believe in?

Akilah, a highly respected priest-scholar in Magi society, considers all his astronomy discoveries well-deserved stepping-stones to a more fulfilling life. But the appearance of a new star challenges his priorities. As Persia totters on the brink of an undesirable king coming to power, Akilah declines a position that could turn that tide. Instead, he studies a star that doesn't appear in any almanac or religious writings. Except Jewish.

When he and his colleagues uncover a few Jewish prophecies linking the star to an eternal king, Akilah becomes the target of Persia's religious and governmental conflicts. Jailed for crimes he didn't commit, Akilah must rely on questionable resources to free himself and reach Jerusalem.

Persia's purists aren't the only ones bent on keeping their country free of Jewish influences. As dangers at home and abroad plunge Akilah and his colleagues into three countries' religious conflicts and circumstances beyond their imagining, Akilah realizes his knowledge of Yeshua could potentially destroy Magi society and its power over Persia's official religion and government. Untrusting of his Council, a thousand miles from aid, and bound in a potentially career-ending contract, Akilah must decide how far he will go to protect what he knows of Yeshua—and whether the cost of his belief is worth the risk.

Get your copy here:

https://scrivenings.link/newstar

Stay up-to-date on your favorite books and authors with our free e-newsletters.

ScriveningsPress.com